Confrontation 9

Taking on the Challenges of Work, Family and Purpose

Dilshad Dayani

Printed in the United States of America
Lead 2 Empower Institute
First Edition, 2014
ISBN: 978-1500544614

*"If you are always trying to be normal,
you will never know how amazing you can be."*

— Maya Angelou

Dedication

******

I dedicate this book with much love, appreciation and gratitude
to the memory of my late parents, Dolly and Aziz,
who sacrificed their comfort to give me a great education and
quietly guided me down the path of compassion.

Part of the Proceeds will be donated to
World Women Global Council a 501c3 nonprofit organization.
Empowering Young Girls and Women Locally and Globally
www.worldwomenglobalcouncil.org

Acknowledgements

First, a big thank you to my family for encouraging me and patiently bearing with me while I took on yet another challenge. I am sincerely grateful to them for understanding my long nights in front of the computer. I'd like to thank my husband Salim, for his continued support, and my children, Tabish and Shazeb, who I consider as my distinguished mentors. Their assistance in helping me pick quotes for the book came after productive debates at the dining table.

I don't think this project would have come to fruition without my mentor and good friend, Greg Campbell, and his faith and belief in me all along the way. The motivation and guidance I received from him has played a significant role in my completion of this project. His support will always be cherished. Speaking of encouragement and inspiration, I am honored and humbled by great female and male leaders and my mentors, who took the time to endorse my book. I extend my deepest gratitude to

- Honorable Congresswoman Eddie Bernice Johnson,

- Dr. Nafis Sadiq, senior policy advisor to the United Nations Secretary General,

- Mary Anne Howland, Founder and President of Global Diversity and Leadership Exchange,

- Bill Wallace, Founder of Success North Dallas and Chairman & CEO at Wallace Companies, Inc., and

- Keith Novick, Chairman of the Hedge Fund Association's (HFA) academic advisory board.

I am deeply indebted to all my friends for sharing my happiness when I started this project, cheering me on when it seemed too difficult to complete. Your energy was amazing! Last but by no means least, my sincere gratitude goes out to Rhiannon and Reina, our editors, and to all those who supported me in the final completion of the book. Their contribution was truly helpful with pertinent revisions and timely suggestions.

And finally, to all whose discussions and insightful wisdom helped me carve my pathways of thoughts and expression, I am humbled by your kindness and pay my deepest gratitude to all of you. I know for sure that without your love, I could not have accomplished it!

****

What Others Are Saying About
CONFRONTATION 9...

"Confrontation 9" is a self-challenging genre- Dilshad offers a thought-provoking approach to success, gender perspective and practical insight, questioning conformity amidst globalization of cultural values. A great read for meaningful lives!

-Congresswoman Eddie Bernice Johnson

*

"Confrontation 9" is an invaluable harvest of practical insights on gender gap, success and conformity. It challenges the readers to reflect on their everyday cultural practices and question the norm to find their true happiness. Dilshad's work has always been an affirming message of self-worth and change.

-Dr. Nafis Sadik,
Special Adviser to the United Nations Secretary-General,
First female director of a United Nations agency.
"One of the most powerful women in the world" (*London Times*)

*

A book of great inspiration and insight on conformity to cultural values. It engages and inspires the reader with the human spirit to redefine his or her own unique Vision of Success and the pathway to make that Vision a reality.

-Bill Wallace,
Founder of Success North Dallas and Chairman
& CEO at Wallace Companies, Inc.

*

Dilshad Dayani has learned the power of asking for what she wants, expecting the universe to deliver it, and sharing her blessings with others. Her book presents her global perspective and illustrates her earnest commitment to self-empowerment. Her words inspire, inform and impact life styles.

-Mary Anne Howland,
Founder, President & Chief Excitement Officer,
Ibis Communications, Inc.
& Founder and CEO, Global Diversity Leadership Exchange

*

All readers, whatever their cultural views, will find much to stimulate their thinking in this book. The everyday nature of conformity paradigm provokes both thought and emotion for questioning the norms. Good educational perspective for our youth to become reflective, observant, and introspective—to one day being professionals of their dreams.

-Keith Novick,
Chairman of the Hedge Fund Association's (HFA)
academic advisory board

****

Contents

Introduction

"Life is beautiful, as long as it consumes you.
When it is rushing through you, life is gorgeous, glorious.
It's when you burn a slow fire and save fuel that life's not worth having."
– DH Lawrence

Do you feel like you are stuck in a maze of repeated
attempts to fix your destiny?

Are you so focused on the happiness of others, you neglect the
search for your own joy and self-fulfillment?

Are your days filled with lengthy to-do lists, responsibilities that
burden you, and obligations that blind your real purpose?

Do you face an inner conflict of
values, traditions, and societal norms?

Y ou are not alone. You may be challenged by a few of the above statements or perhaps all of them. Whatever you are trying to avoid won't go away until you confront it. There are many reasons for not finding fulfillment and happiness in our lives as we construct our realities. The truth is that we ignore the pursuit of our own contentment because it just seems like a cliché, and eventually, this pursuit becomes our greatest obstacle and fear.

Our own lack of will and focus is the single source (and the only obstacle) preventing each one of us from becoming our true selves. As we witness on a daily basis how the voice of doubt quietly but more aggressively overrules our personal truth and wisdom, we also experience our vulnerability and embrace doubt more frequently. The echo of distrust suggests we aren't good enough or aren't courageous enough to stand up for what we believe in. How many times have we brushed aside the thought of embracing contentment as our top priority? Simply put, we are letting self-imposed limits or the way we were raised restrain us from our true path and what we can do. We blame it on culture, faith, family, or circumstance. We whisper this to ourselves quite often, don't we?

I first came to America from Pakistan when I arrived in Los Angeles in the early nineties. I had been exposed to this country through movies, television, and friends who had visited America, so culture shock on a surface level wasn't such an issue. However, I noticed the stark contrasts between where I'd grown up and my new home right away. I was grateful my daily life would now include electricity 24/7 and water shortages wouldn't be such a prevalent problem. I was also quite surprised to see the word "choices" stretched to the point where it would confuse people when ordering a meal or dessert. Witnessing such sharp disparities and finding meaningful conclusions to them was extremely difficult, especially when one's youth was spent watching children and women dying or being abused over a piece of bread. Above all, it was amazing to see children in school and not begging on the streets.

Girls and women could wear anything and had the freedom to walk and talk as they pleased. As I waited on the bus every day after work, I would question again and again how promoting basic human rights was a challenge in certain countries. I felt emotionally conflicted over these realizations, but on the flipside, I felt blessed and privileged as a woman. I saw and became inspired by the accomplishments and fearlessness of women around me.

After I arrived and began settling in, simple facts changed my lifestyle. Though, I had grown used to the fact that *masis* and *naukars* (maids and servants) were an indispensable part of life in Pakistan and India. However, in America, I observed how houses didn't need to be cleaned every day. From food choices to clothing, and entertainment to work attitudes, a variety of mental battles raged within me, particularly when it came to the traditions, customs, and values of my newfound home.

I was constantly questioning how I could make everyone happy, especially my husband and in-laws, as I was a newlywed at the time. I wondered how I would be able to create a balance between the two value systems and the challenges that arose from this conflict to address my work, family, and innate purpose, while also struggling to determine what it meant to be a proud American woman. What would it take to live like a comfortable, mainstream member of society? To what extent would I be taken negatively if I did certain things or communicated differently? Would my accent, attire, traditions, or attitude set me apart from everyone else? Would it make me feel like a stranger in my new home in Los Angeles?

The barrage of questions simmered in my mind. The quest had just begun for adventure, experimentation and struggle with conflicting notions. This was America, where dreams come true and the word "ordinary" had tremendous power over an individual, more so than any other word in the dictionary. You see, being "ordinary" is a double-edged sword—you can fit in if you are ordinary, but you also don't get the chance to stand out from the crowd. I realized how some South Asian community members had done well materially, and it was precisely because they strove not to be typical, "ordinary" immigrants in America that they succeeded. No doubt, strong values of self-discipline and hard work turned their dreams into realities.

As I started embracing the possibility of a doubt-free perspective, my dream to be a strong woman in this country started to develop. It was like being reborn. Enjoying my liberty to wear what I liked and to do what my heart aspired without fear, shame, guilt, or threat was simply peaceful. Being a woman and waking up with limitless possibilities can be scary, but truly intoxicating. I could now navigate daily in a safe and serene state of mind.

These were my factual observations as a human being, and in no way am I implying that one country has superiority over another. The library of my experiences spoke from my heart in a sad and helpless way. I was upset how corrupt people in leadership could create miserable lives for the masses. I had experienced the political and religious ban on various rights for women in India, Pakistan, and Bangladesh—the three countries of my childhood—and I could feel the pain. My questions became a voice of advocacy and a refuge to seek peace. How would my resources and the power of education end suffering?

Would I be able to create a balance in my life by taking on the challenges of work, family, and purpose? How did I wish to determine how much **emotional and psychological** baggage I could carry? How would I redefine success so that it completes the equation of contentment, faith, compassion, and interests? What would I need to become a true American citizen?

Learning about my evolving self, the cultural ideals, religious teachings, and aspects of my personality created a silent war that waged between my years of mental conditioning and the way things were now in my life. I did things a certain way in the past, because that was simply how it was done. But now, things were different. I encountered a phase of confrontation, my freedom of expression at odds with the cultural norms or conventions I grew up with.

I'd grown accustomed to these norms for the better part of my life, and they became who I was. My faith always taught me to be of value and service to others. This true awakening of the soul integrated into a lifestyle choice, taking fruition in my parents' lives; even though they had meager means, they made up for their lack of material wealth with compassionate hearts.

My ideas of guilt, family inclusiveness, and community approval based on cultural and personal values were still strong. I was embracing a society where logic, in terms of religion and cultural norms, could be questioned openly and freely, without reservations or judgments. Until now, this concept was foreign to me, because oftentimes this could cost you your life if displayed publicly in my home country. When I was a student, I was unable to approach the principal and ask why certain university procedures were unfair, or why particular students were tremendously favored over others. When I would try to voice the need for fairness by raising an argument or taking an action, my friends would scare me to death by speculating the outcome of my protests. They would convince me how it would lead to bigger chaos and life-threatening issues that would end nowhere. It was just the way things were.

Once in America, I honestly wished I could deliver the freedom I was blessed with to all the women in the world and help them discover the immense power and courage that lie within them. My ambitious nature was not ready to give up in the face of challenges, and I was determined to find alternate routes and forge new trails.

Consider this book to be a journey to your own awakening, on which you get the chance to become who you want, without hesitation or personal boundaries preventing you.

And, as we walk together, I will share a few personal challenges with you. The most interesting insight you will notice as we journey is how we all share a common bond. We play the role of generous, fearless, and capable advisers ready to offer ourselves to others, allowing them to see their strength and the road of reality to their dreams. However, we are all scared to confront our own limitations, and we fear our weaknesses. We like to bury our heads in the sand and wait for luck, a miracle, or some spell to break for our reality to blossom.

In the following pages, you'll learn how diverse concepts of success in our society, built by the media and through cultural conditioning, can inhibit and blur your priorities. You will see how they limit your ability to define and experience the greatness within you. We each search for meaningful lives, yet feel helpless because we have forgotten our power to change things. Many of us have allowed circumstances to block goals we've set for ourselves. Perhaps someone close to you doubted your potential or held you back by focusing on your weaknesses and setting the stage of uncertainty for you.

Often, people around you don't share your dreams, because they do not have a vested interest in the outcome. Let me repeat that again—they do not have a vested interest in the outcome. What does this mean? Simply put, your success isn't their vision. They are not committed to working with you to produce the end result, to achieve your hopes and dreams, because the majority of human beings possess a "what's in it for me" mentality. When you have a dream, a goal, a real purpose, you are 100 percent fully invested in the outcome. Once you are invested in the outcome, you own it and become completely committed to the results. When you are 100 percent devoted to a goal from beginning to end, you gain the power to see it through until you become the person YOU want to be.

Appreciate yourself for who you truly are . . .
because of your flaws, not in spite of them.

"We're all human beings, but some of us are more sophisticated at
covering our flaws. We're just smart enough to lie
to ourselves that everything is OK."
– Mehmet Oz

In my early days of transitioning, I remember chatting with a friend in Los Angeles who asked me something that really made me think about self-criticism and being compassionate to oneself. I guess she had heard me talking about my old home in Pakistan and my struggle to find a place in my new home here in America. She inquired, "If there was one thing you could say to a friend who was being critical of herself, one bit of advice, what would it be?" I thought about this long and hard, because her question really struck a chord with me.

A good number of us are critical of ourselves because of social conditioning. Our desire to compete is directly tied to our survival. For the most part, we live in a society where we are expected to be strong and flawless. We are constantly bombarded and encouraged by the media and others around us to be our own worst critics. "Be the best, do better, and never admit defeat" is ingrained into our minds. The need for perfection and the yearning to be a winner cloud many of our pursuits today. We either lie about how much we excel in a particular area or dwell on areas where we falter so heavily that they become hindrances to our self-growth.

After really thinking about how I wanted to reply to my friend, I simply said, "I would tell her that she is simply picking up garbage and throwing it at herself, self-sabotaging by putting herself down to the point of obsession. Having no self-compassion is the biggest roadblock to our potential. In order to experience clarity of mind and soul, it is important we don't lie to ourselves."

We're human; we're allowed to have flaws. Our progressive nature gives us the capacity to learn from our mistakes, seizing the opportunity to use past errors to build on our strengths for the future.

Just for a moment, I want you to imagine how your life would be if you were born absolutely perfect, if you lived your life free of mistakes and excelled in absolutely everything you attempted. You might wonder what is so bad about that. Well, let me relay a piece of research conducted by Brené Brown, a professor at the University of Houston, Graduate College of Social Work. She spent ten years studying vulnerability, shame, authenticity, and courage. Her research indicated we get sucked into perfection for one very simple reason: we believe perfection will protect us and shield us from life's burdens and fears. Perfectionism is the belief that if we live, look, and act perfectly, we can minimize or avoid the pain of blame, judgment, and shame.

So, how do we find the courage and compassion to love ourselves, despite our imperfections? When do we realize we are good enough, worthy of love and happiness? And why are we frozen by the fear of what other people think or say about us? Brown's studies signify that we have a craving to belong and to be loved. We are biologically and mentally hardwired to feel comfortable when we are part of the "group" and accepted. When this doesn't happen, we begin to break down. We experience pain and discomfort, and may even begin to feel physically ill. In short, we suffer on a very deep level.

The research interviews also revealed one core issue that

separated individuals who felt they belonged from those who were striving for that connection: **self-worth.** The truth is, if we want to belong and be loved, we have to feel we are worthy of it. However, the common belief is that we will only be worthy if we ignore who we are now, take care of our flaws, and become a more perfect person.

I'll deserve to be loved when I lose weight.
I'll deserve to be loved when I can have a baby.
I'll deserve to be loved when I find the right person.
I'll deserve to be loved when I can kick my bad habits.
I'll deserve to be loved when I am good enough for my partner.
I'll deserve to be loved when my parents approve of me.
I'll deserve to be loved when I am a success.

The truth is, we are worthy of love right now. We deserve to be loved and accepted this very minute, not some time in the future. You are enough! You deserve to be happy, and you deserve to be in control of your journey. You do have the courage and strength to be loved today!

Confrontation 9 will help you identify traits we all find in our internal "drawers." Perhaps, just like those proverbial skeletons in our closets, we deny our negative attributes and weaknesses and tuck them away in our "drawers" because we just don't want to validate, change, or encounter the uncomfortable task of self-development. We'd rather ignore it and be comfortable blocking our true potential. Maybe this is due to cultural beliefs and conditioning, or perhaps we are hindered by societal norms we've allowed to dominate our true purpose. This book is about finding the unique, healthy, and fulfilled place in your heart and mind. It is the discovery of the cozy spot we long for in chilly weather. It reveals roadblocks so we can hear the voice of choice and develop the patience to listen to intuition. It will build and activate the cognitive tools within us in a profound way.

Through this book, I attempt to help you discover something that has been part of your rich potential all these years—your inner strength and your much-awaited destiny. You may be thinking, "Are there tools to help me?" Yes, the tool kit takes you through simple steps called **CLEAR 5.** This 5-step process cognitively helps you identify and map your problems so you can simplify them for desired outcomes in everyday decision making.

Through stories, research, and relevant ideas, you will be in a position to question, analyze, and arrive at some conclusions about yourself and the cultural values you want to belong to. However, more significantly, this process offers you the opportunity to leave behind a legacy. This is an amazing gift for your family, your children, or the institution to which you have given your life. You get the chance to pass on a value system as a human being with the highest honor, gratitude, and awareness of why you are here and what you aspire to be. Ultimately, *Confrontation 9* attempts to stir the power within you to experience meaningful success, happiness, and courage with utmost clarity and your value based culture map.

Writing this book has been a cathartic process. It has given me the opportunity to see past the fear of judgment and self-doubt that often plague our lives. Most of all, it has allowed me to see through my lens of experiences, struggles, challenges and joy. It has offered me the confidence and clarity of purpose to bring me closer to the most precious, breathless adventure we are blessed with: **LIFE!**

Oftentimes, a single book has a unique power in its concept—in its message—to affect positive change in those who read it. Let this book lead you toward a path of accomplishment, fulfillment, and exceptional heights. Let this reading free you from all the limitations and bring you where you are destined to be!

You are on a journey of life, full of challenges. Allow me to share with you how I confronted the obstacles in my life, leapt over them, and gained meaningful success while redefining my destiny. From my heart to yours—enjoy the path that truly belongs to you.

Warning: This book is only intended for those who are truly ready to question the norm and understand the source of our values and the factors that drive us. How can we break barriers to seek happiness and self-fulfillment? In this book, you will be asked to challenge yourself, to push your own self-imposed boundaries, whether created by culture or any other system dominating your script of life.

Are you ready to analyze societal norms and become the person you want to be? Do you want to address the challenges of work, family, and purpose with clarity and conviction? If you are determined to decode the true path to leave behind those self-imposed limitations that have held you back for so long, then let's walk together ....

TO REVEAL THE REAL YOU!

Chapter 1

From Conformity to Clarity

*"Once conform, once do what other people do because they do it,
and a lethargy steals over all the finer nerves and faculties of the
soul. She becomes all outer show and inward emptiness;
dull, callous, and indifferent."*
—*Virginia Woolf*

T here is one fact we must keep in mind: we are all born wholly unique. Each of us has an individualistic character, inherent from our very first breath, yet somewhere along the way, we begin trying to be like others. We strive for "normalcy," and in the process, a vast majority of us lose our originality. We forget we have every right to be ourselves in the context of our passions, dreams and value systems. The truth is, we surrender the ability to make decisions that set us apart from the crowd and because of this, and we fail to see our extraordinary potential.

Did you ever do something against your better judgment, simply because everyone else was doing it?

Are there times when you aren't being yourself around others because they might think you're "different"?

When was the last time you stood up for yourself and actually did something you felt was right, even if it went against the status quo?

In many respects, conformity has become an epidemic. Rather than striving to be our best and do everything with our true potential and power, we allow conformity to limit us. It becomes a boundary we are afraid to cross for fear of what might happen if we do.

Why We Choose Conformity

As I was beginning to acclimate to my new society, the issue of conformity was an everyday challenge. While I began to learn and understand familial customs in America, and gained insight into certain traditions, I could feel myself struggling against the discomfort I felt as cultures clashed. I was confused by the two value systems that I now held: one focused on the individual, and the other embraced group approval and welfare. The challenge was finding a balance between the two and determining how much group interest one should sacrifice in order to meet personal comfort, dreams, and ambitions. I was not taught to think or place myself before the group, such as my family or people in need. I ended up plagued with guilt if I claimed preferential status and put myself before the needs of others. The conflict was a daily exercise in justifying behavior. However, my quest to redefine my principles ultimately gave me clarity about the clashing value systems inside me.

It was a Saturday afternoon, and I walked into my friend's salon. She is a great hairstylist. In fact, I consider her to be a magician when it comes to crafting the perfect look and style, an important part of the image-driven lives in our society. I was at her visionary studio and believed she deserved every square inch of the space. Having a dream salon was one of her greatest accomplishments. She was very proud of the fact that she finally built up her client list to the point where she could start her own business.

I was very happy for her and wanted to celebrate her achievement and joy. I brought compliments and gifts for her soaring success. I sat there admiring and chatting with her, until she had to attend to a walk-in client. As I watched her, I noticed there was a sort of anxious, yet revolutionary spirit in the conversation she was having with the client.

Client: I want to go for something completely new and different. This style is too boring for me now. It's been so long since I've changed my look.

My Friend: Okay, well, let's see. You always wear your hair straight and blonde and right at your shoulders. So, we could bring it up to just under your ears, add some layers to give it a bit more body, and add some lowlights for depth and contrast? That will be very different and frame your face nicely, I think.

Client: Oh no, I couldn't cut my hair short. It has to stay long. And . . . I don't know about layers, none of my friends have them. Besides, I wouldn't even know how to take care of them. And low lights? That's too extreme. In fact, I have to admit that the whole idea frightens me a bit. How about we just stick with a trim?

It was one of those seemingly mundane conversations encountered in daily life. The situation loudly described the idea of conformity and social norms. The woman was enthusiastic to change her look, to try something different. Change, as we know, is lovely in thought but quite frightening in reality. The mere mention of alterations to her hairstyle sent the woman into a panic, even though that was exactly what she had stepped into the salon for. I saw this as an analogy and said to myself, she is not different. We have all done this, haven't we? If not with our hairstylist, perhaps with someone else. At some point in our lives, we have desired to be different, but then second-guessed ourselves when the time came, or we were too scared to actually make it happen.

Change is one of the most difficult occurrences in life for many, including myself. From a very early age, I had to make a concerted effort to speak my mind in front of my parents. When I did, I ended up being the black sheep for not conforming like the rest of my siblings. In my South Asian culture, submissiveness is synonymous to being good, kind, and polite, so it is considered one of the best qualities a woman can have. Or, shall I say, submissiveness is a part of social expectations set by elders and practiced widely in many parts of the world. Respect for authority is also tied to submissiveness in many cultures.

In my experience, gender conformity is yet another major challenge. It places a veil on women's place in the world, as women are consistently relegated to second place, and it serves to shut down the most creative forces. It is absolutely one of the main reasons so much abuse is unaccounted for and why so many women fall short of their true potential. A woman learns to accept this conformity as her destiny or uses it as a survival mechanism because until very recently, when campaigns for women's rights began to flourish, very few people seemed to question the brutality. Girls are taught to conform and assume without challenging authority. As a young girl, I began to see how my mental capacities were discounted simply because I was physically vulnerable.

Daring to become someone different from what is considered or accepted as normal can be altogether terrifying. Standing up for what you truly believe in and voicing your thoughts amongst a crowd of people who have differing opinions and beliefs are two of the greatest obstacles to overcome. We tell ourselves how we might offend someone else or be seen as strange, so we hold our tongues and distract our minds.

Women tend to create comfort zones where there is less questioning, less critical thinking and less respect. Eventually, women find that they have fewer rights and less equality on their path to survival and success. Many women who embark upon this journey rewire their brains, as well as their hearts, and begin to happily accept inequality. They begin to believe tolerance is for the greater good and attribute it to destiny to the point where they associate it with grace and dignity. The cultural perspective reinforces, and in many cases provides, immunity against the guilt that often comes with this kind of conformity.

The simple truth can be observed in our daily lives. The majority of women have grown accustomed to quietly staying in the background. We prefer taking our thoughts, our ideas, and our beliefs home with us. Instead of being publically vocal about what we believe in and sharing opinions about a particular aspect of life, we hop onto our computers and tell complete strangers because we feel protected when sitting behind those screens.

The chance of others finding out we are different can be terrifying. We want to take control of our vulnerability and remain safe and normal, so we tell people what they want to hear. Then we monitor how much change we make in our life and ensure the increments are so small no one will notice or be offended by them.

Why? Because we convince ourselves it's safer that way. Except in the back of our minds, we know it's boring. We know deep down we can do better or be different, and we aren't really happy with the status quo in our hearts.

We live in a society where individualism is touted as a positive attribute, but is actually frowned upon in many situations and environments. For example, corporations require employees to follow a handbook telling them how to act, what to do and how to do it—flexibility or creativity in many areas is not encouraged. There are entire housing developments where you'll find each home is the same and everyone living in those homes is expected to maintain their lawns and paint their houses in a similar way.

We all follow society's rules and distract ourselves from the fact that we live in a world of mundane procedures by making small talk with neighbors and friends. Sometimes we wonder if we are saying anything of value, but we are simply too afraid of what that might lead to. In essence, the majority of us are wasting our lives out of fear of what might happen if we dared to be different.

A Few Factors that Influence Conformity:

There are a variety of different factors influencing conformity. If you are able to recognize which situations typically generate instances of conformity in your life, you will be able to identify and understand the nature of your behavior and the behavior of others around you. You may perhaps, through right questioning, come full circle with clarity of thought and actions. Here are a few of the most common factors that have a direct impact on conformity:

1. Group settings. It's been shown that group sizes between three to five people exhibit the most conformity. When there are less than three people in a group, conformity is greatly decreased (Bond 2005).

2. Disagreement. Conformity greatly increases if someone in a group disagrees or cannot decide upon a particular stance. Conformity can be reduced from 97 percent to 36 percent when there is at least one individual who disagrees (Allen & Levine 1971).

3. The need to belong. The need to feel like you are part of a group is yet another factor that influences conformity. As a matter of fact, the need to belong is so strong it may lead us to behave or do things in the exact opposite way than those who are in another group (David & Turner 1996).

4. Mood. The current state of our mood can factor into conformity. It's believed that we more easily conform when we are in a good mood rather than a bad mood (Tong et al. 2007). There is even evidence how the "fear-relief" technique can make someone conform. Using this technique, you would force someone to become afraid and then relieve those fears. This is thought to make them more likely to conform to your beliefs and ideas (Dolinski & Nawrat 1998).

5. Approval. A majority of us feel some need for approval. This will often make us feel better about ourselves and boost our self-esteem. When you care what someone thinks of you, and try to be what is considered normal, you are conforming.

6. Culture. There are certain cultures, such as those found in Asian countries, where nonconformity is seen as a sign of social defiance (Kim & Markus 1999). In some of these cultures, it has been observed that people fear for their lives if they question authority. On the other hand, Western cultures typically have more individualistic attitudes. As such, people from these cultures are typically less likely to conform. In fact, research has shown that "collectivist cultures" have conformity rates between 25 percent and 58 percent, while "individualist cultures" have conformity rates between 14 percent and 39 percent (Smith & Bond 1993).

7. Social "norms". How many times have you done something just because you thought it was done by someone else? This is an example of conforming based upon social norms. A vast majority of us are strongly influenced by how others might behave when in the same situation as us (Cialdini 2001).

As you can see, there are a myriad of factors that influence our choice to conform. The important thing to remember is that the power of conformity reshapes who we are and what we will become. Research has shown that there is a relationship between our brains and social influences. Our brain actually adapts to make room for conformity. We are all designed to conform on some level, but the question we must ask ourselves is: how much and at what cost? How far do we wish to stretch the notion of conformity before it starts to dictate our lives entirely?

One thing is for certain—no matter the person or situation—this submissive mindset to always bow down can easily sneak up on you. You won't even know you are conforming, and that is why it is both dangerous and addictive. You may have been young, hopeful, and filled with crazy creativity and aspirations for how you were going to change the world. Then, slowly but surely, you conformed. Someone came along and said, "You aren't allowed to drink tea; we all drink coffee with two creams." So you stopped drinking tea and switched to coffee with two creams. Then another person whispered, "You can't wear blue socks, you have to wear white."

So you threw out your blue socks and purchased white ones. Before you know it, you are just like everyone else— wearing, drinking, and doing things you don't even really want to do. You are no longer unique, the one who had such high hopes, but just another one amidst the many. Time slips by; you've lost yourself somewhere along the way, and the scariest part is, you didn't even notice it was happening.

Now, you find yourself all grown up, trying to stay afloat and making sure everyone else is happy. But the most important question to ask yourself is: are you happy? It is extremely important to perform a "Conformist Test Scan" (CT-SCAN) of our mental capacities and see if we are able to confront and tolerate the critical questioning. Chances are, we don't want to invade our self-prophesies or disturb our self-esteem. This is primarily because the hardest thing for us to do is to remove ourselves from our current mold and design an entirely new cookie cutter to work with. It requires effort, we risk splits in our social groups, and above all, we must have the courage to stand and present our own case to ourselves before we are brave enough to show it to the world. In other words, we like to create barricades so that we don't end up in discomfort.

When was the last time you did something for yourself that pushed you outside of your comfort zone?

How long has it been since you've contemplated what you really wanted to do with your life?

Are you able to answer these questions, or have you been conforming for so long you have forgotten your own strengths and hopes? Is it because you are afraid to challenge or question your own cultural norms, traditions and belief systems? Or could it be family value systems based on legacies, traditions, and honor trails that stand in your way? The amazing news is that even if you have given into conformity, your true self is still there. It's just waiting for you to rediscover it. It's waiting for you to realize and embrace the fact that you have free will. We just need to allow our true light to wake up, shine, and seize the opportunity.

How Corporate Culture Encourages Conformity

"The opposite of courage in our society
is not cowardice, it's conformity."
—Rollo May

In many respects, the corporate world stifles our

individualism and uniqueness. If you take a close look at the design of its structures, it's apparent that the corporate world relies upon the idea of conformity. Each employee is asked to be just like every other employee. They must do the same things in the same way without question, wear the same clothing, and stick to the handbook when dealing with particular situations. In this way, we become products of an assembly line.

Thinking for oneself or doing things differently is often frowned upon, and as such, this conformity inevitably robs us of our true selves. The corporate world also tends to create a strong web of corporate normalcy, and one can easily become mesmerized by physical wealth and net worth. In fact, this can happen to such an extent that it drains our ability to strive for anything more than climbing the corporate ladder. However, we often do this without evaluating the cost in terms of our own personal timelines. In this process, our true identity and purpose take second place, and we get disillusioned by our job. I often recall a story that was told to me by a good friend. It reminds me of how the corporate structure emphasizes adherence to procedures and absolute compliance, often compromising creativity and innovation.

My friend's neighbor had worked for a large corporation some years back and was asked to sit in on a few interviews the human resources manager was holding one afternoon. One by one the candidates came into the office and were asked a series of questions, each of them designed to gauge the individual's loyalty, skill level, and work ethic, among other things.

The last candidate, dressed in brightly colored clothing, came into the room and obviously stood out. While the other interviewees had worn suits that were shades of gray, black, and dark blue, this gentleman had on a bright purple suit with a vibrant yellow tie. My friend noticed this difference in attire, but didn't think anything of it at the time. The man was still dressed professionally, just not like the other candidates. The man answered all of the questions perfectly. He acted the part of a businessman, was confident, and his credentials were far better than those of the other candidates. When the man left the room, my friend turned to the Human Resources manager and said, "Well, I guess we know who's a shoo-in for the job. That last candidate was perfect for our company, right?"

The Human Resources Manager replied sarcastically, "Do you work for the same company as I do? You know quite well that if we hire him he won't last a week. Who comes to an interview looking like that, anyway?"

My friend was a bit taken aback by the response. Even though the candidate was far more qualified, he wasn't going to be offered the position simply because he didn't fit into the image the company had in mind. He didn't look like one of their employees. Simply put, he didn't fit into the picture the company had of the ideal candidate.

This stuck in my friend's mind, mainly because the company seemed to be totally unaware of the fact that this particular candidate had so much to offer. He could have brought his unique talents and innovative, out-of-the-box solutions to the table to further collective success. However, they were unwilling to see past his unconventional wardrobe. The problem with conformity in the corporate world is that it hinders not only the success of the company, but also the individual capacity for creativity. You have to fit into the mold the company has set for you, and leaving that mold may cost you your job.

For instance, exhibiting creativity is often seen as being nonconformist. You often have to say farewell to structure and cultural norms if you really want to express yourself freely. However, many of the basic aspects of society, such as governmental institutions and our education system, are founded upon conformity, and more often than not, their slowing progress is the result of confined policy structures and rigid procedural settings.

Now the question arises: how much conformity is essential for a peaceful and progressive life? How much should we conform in order to retain stability in our home, workplace, and community? Are you willing to be a clone and live your life based upon the standards and ideas of others? Or are you going to break away from the norm? How can you achieve your own definition of success in terms of work, family, and purpose?

The answer lies in creating guidelines to follow a clear map that can nurture flexibility and imagination. This allows for an innovative working space in which individuals can thrive. The fine line must be a systematic and cognitive approach, which I call "creative gravity." Organizational laws must not conflict with personal expression of ingenuity, but rather, complement it.

However, this approach also calls for the fine-tuning of an institution's faith and trust. How do we manage it while keeping the best forces in play? The first catalyst to ignite change in your behavior is identifying your definition of meaningful success. This will be the paradigm shift of your focus for building the value map. Let me leave you with some common insights on conformity that will perhaps paint a clearer picture.

Examples of Conformity

- A teenager dresses in a certain style because he wants to fit in with the rest of the guys in his social group.

- A 20-year-old college student drinks at a sorority party because all her friends are doing it, and she does not want to be the odd one out.

- A woman reads a book for her book club and really enjoys it. When she attends her book club meeting, the other members all disliked the book. Rather than go against the group opinion, she simply agrees with the others that the book was terrible.

- Chinese parents are not necessarily driven to control their children; instead, they are expected to teach their children how to maintain harmony with others. For example, emotional expression is considered harmful to one's health and relationships, and children are encouraged to avoid it. Such practices create the context for "saving face." This value or behavior is related to shame because it rewards conformity to society's expectations for propriety and harmony (Van Campen and Russell 2010).

- A student is unsure about the answer to a particular question posed by the teacher. When another student in the class provides an answer, the confused student concurs with the answer, believing that the other student is smarter and better informed.

Remember, the media contributes to this emphasis on conformity by perpetuating the value of fitting in and feeding your perceptions on a daily basis. In order to realize your worth, you must be courageous and confident enough to challenge the value placed on conformity, which is essentially a concept based on ignorance and popular views. The process will create mindfulness and generate the power of clarity to create a unique value-based culture map.

Chapter 2

Recognizing Gender Conformity to Redefine Success

"Men go abroad to wonder at the heights of mountains, at the huge waves of the sea, at the long courses of the rivers, at the vast compass of the ocean, at the circular motions of the stars, and they pass by themselves without wondering."
–St. Augustine

The problem many of us face today is that we associate the acquisition of knowledge with self-awareness. We assume we will be able to better understand ourselves if we learn more and build upon our skill sets. We are no longer a collection of experiences and life lessons learned, but rather, are simply representative of what culture has made us and what books have taught us. We ignore who we are and what we have become. The truth is that there is no substitute for self-reflection.

What does success mean to you? Is it a big house in the hills and an expensive car, or is it being happy and fulfilled in all aspects of your life? Does the thought of earning enough to take vacations all over the globe motivate you, or do you focus more on the less tangible pleasures in life? Learning about your own version of happiness is the key to actually achieving success on your own terms, without cultural or societal expectations standing in your way. ***Your gender should not be a boundary for your success!***

For some, achieving success means having all facets of your life in perfect harmony and balance. For others, success entails being happy, even if that means you don't have a dime to your name. There are even certain individuals who believe that being truly successful involves being as productive as possible in every way imaginable.

The redefinition of success in your life means that you are able to transform your perception into meaning. In many respects, today's definition, for a vast majority of our population, is to strive for some lofty idea of success, which has been set by society as a whole. The simple and unfortunate truth is that we are all, to some degree, experiencing the world in a muted way. Instead of finding joy by doing what we love and fulfilling our own purpose, we are trying to seek out happiness by doing what others expect us to do. We are judging our success based on how much we are able to obtain and how much money we earn, because that is how society measures fulfillment and joy. No doubt, this type of fulfillment is quite capable of temporarily distracting us, but eventually, the emptiness comes to question us in different ways.

The word "fulfillment" is thrown around quite often these days. In fact, it's used so frequently that it's lost a bit of its meaning in many contexts. However, when I say "fulfillment," I mean leading a life that is happy, joyful, and abundant. If you are fulfilled, then you can honestly say without hesitation that you have achieved your own sort of success, and that you have clarity of purpose in every way imaginable. Only through achieving fulfillment can you claim to be truly successful.

When I first immigrated to America with my husband, I was well aware of the fact that I would have to undergo a rather extreme adjustment period. After all, I was raised in an Asian culture, wherein we are encouraged to conform and blend in with the crowd, so to speak. In America, however, I encountered a society that was by and large individualistic. Yet, as I became more accustomed to American society, it became increasingly clear how the media plays a large role in driving the idea of conformity and encouraging the pursuit of perfection—an ideal that is governed by others' opinions and social norms.

Moreover, shortly after I arrived, I had to endure a personal loss that made the adjustment even more difficult for me. I suffered two miscarriages; both of which left me devastated and unsure if I would be able to cope. Added to this was the fact that I was virtually alone in a strange, new country, trying my best to acclimate to an unfamiliar culture. I was lonely, to say the least, and the life I was leading was now filled with foreign traditions and people with whom I barely shared any common bonds.

I remember vividly that day when someone told me (after I had lost my baby) that I should "look at the bright side" and "resume my work routine now." I couldn't fathom why someone would say such a thing at such a time. I knew that the person probably meant well, but they were simply unaware of how I was grieving so deeply for my loss that work just didn't play into the equation. To me, being successful had nothing to do with how much money I had, but my family and having a baby in my arms meant the world to me. Having a job and earning an income were surely factors that determined my success as an immigrant; however, at the time of my loss, a home and a baby were more significant to me and more in line with my modest idea of success—one that I had brought with me to America.

The fact that I was married and that my basic financial needs were met did shift my entire focus toward my realization of being a mother, and many women who come from different cultures do not feel that success. Happiness and peace can be equated with jobs outside the home, and personal worth can be all about six-figure incomes or climbing the corporate ladder.

Because of these cultural truths, the communal feeling of success and worth is what American individualistic culture is devoid of, and that is why so many motivational and coaching books are consumed by our culture than any other. The American self-help industry is worth roughly $1 billion, and books alone bring in $776 million of that total. According to Marketdata Enterprises, a market research and consulting firm, approximately 70 percent of the consumers who purchase self-help or motivational products such as books, seminars, and workshops are affluent American women (Marketdata Enterprises 2012). The reason why, in this day and age, there are so many self-help books being sold to the American public is because so many of us are unhappy. We are looking for ways to find contentment, to find a remedy for the dissatisfaction with our lives, and to find hope.

It often feels to me as though a significant segment of our society is living a life as though they are sitting in the crowd, watching events helplessly unfold on the stage. They are too afraid to actually get up and be heard, to share their voice, and to become a participant in the play. Instead, they leave that to the actors, the ones who are brave enough to get up there and become involved in the story. It is only the actors who can honestly say they are living, not just getting by, and can become self-aware by trying to understand themselves and the world around them.

Even though I had to experience loss and endure some loneliness when starting my life in a new country. However, I am proud to say like many of you that I have continually tried to bring the best out of me in the face of the many constraints. I challenged myself to learn the environment and the people I belonged to now, making a life for my family, myself and serving others. It was difficult to allow my experiences to open my eyes to possibilities. By helping others in this process, I saw many who experienced the same transitional phases. Nonetheless, I am proud of this country that has blessed me with freedom, peace, and a great education.

I won't let social norms or conformity keep me from being happy or fulfilled, nor will I let self-imposed limitations prevent me from grasping my true nature and emotions. I never want to be a spectator in the crowd. I won't settle for that!

Life is meant to be lived on the stage, taking an active part in one's life and seizing every opportunity for self-discovery that comes our way.

Was I able to come up with a completely different definition of success, or was I redefining success to suit my culturally influenced frame of mind? In my case, after a lot of pondering and reanalyzing my priorities and goals, I decided to journey with a new idea of success. We all redefine success and value systems as we grow and evolve. For example, in our early twenties, we may place a higher value on work and furthering our careers, but when we get married and have children, our priorities are reshaped to reflect the changes in our familiar responsibilities. Similarly, my cultural values and my faith began to juxtapose the new frame of mind I had developed in this new environment that I now lived in and admired. My priority was to stretch the freedom of thought and understand things from an objective perspective, instead of always seeing the world solely through the lens of my culture and faith. And this is how I redefined and reconstructed my own definition of success as I journeyed through life.

As you may have observed, when we talk about success, we cannot ignore the metrics used by both genders to define success.

The question we need to ask is: are these metrics the same or are they different? To what extent do they impact our lifestyle choices, in terms of priorities?

The view from the top...

How men define success:
A survey conducted by LinkedIn and Citi found that about 79 percent of men associate success with being in a good marriage.

Of the 1,023 participants involved in the study, 86 percent of them stated that "having it all" meant also having children. Roughly 50 percent of the men also mentioned that a work-life balance was important in life. For these men, having a family took priority over everything else, as has been the case for centuries (Drexler 2013).

How women define success:

Women also participated in the same Citi and LinkedIn study, and only 73 percent of them said that they equated having children with being successful, while 66 percent of the women stated that they associated a healthy marriage with success (Drexler 2013). These lower numbers are important, because they also coincide with another important fact—according to Forbes, women are the ones earning more college degrees now. In fact, about 58 percent of the degrees earned worldwide are by women. With that being said, only about 4 percent of the world's largest companies are run by women CEOs (Goudreau 2012).

These statistics illustrate a very important fact—that women are beginning to not only just associate success with families and marriage as much as men do in this day and age, but also strongly tie success to careers. Men believe that having children and a happy marriage are the most important things in life, while women are slowly but surely starting to shift to a work-centered life. Success no longer means just having a family for women, but also having a rewarding career.

With only 4 percent of the world's largest companies run by female CEOs, it also shows that women are still much undervalued in the work place. Many cultural norms dictate that women should be happy raising a family and supporting their husbands, and this is reflected in not only their paychecks, which are typically far less than their male counterparts, but also the respect they garner in their professional lives.

Most people who are deemed as "normal" work nine-to-five jobs, which often don't really make them happy. They are trying to stay afloat any way they can and are too busy to be concerned with finding joy in their lives. They are trying so desperately to be successful, to make their fortune, and to be loved by everyone that they fail to grasp one of the most important concepts in life: being unique is our birthright, and it's through the development of our core being that we are led to life's real purpose, bringing contentment and abundance along with us. Ask yourself some difficult questions such as:

- When was the last time you did something for yourself, even though you knew that it might not please others?

- When did you last do something just because you wanted to, instead of doing it because you wanted to try to fit in with the crowd?
- When was the last time you took time for yourself, enjoyed it, and didn't feel guilty afterwards?

If you take a closer look at our world today, you'll probably notice that we have all become obsessed with the notion of acting, thinking, and looking like everyone else. Standing out is associated with being "odd" or "eccentric," while fitting in with the cookie-cutter image of how you should behave and appear in public is the new normal. We are all trying so hard to make others like us that we may lose sight of whether or not we really like ourselves.

In essence, we have each split ourselves into two different people. There is the person we show the world, and then there is the person we truly are, deep within ourselves. A vast majority of us would never dream of showing ourselves to those around us while we are in public. It is only when we are alone that we can be who we really are, without worrying about if someone will like us or not. The problem with this is that we can never be entirely whole. We must always divide our self and our energy between these two identities. As such, we can never be fulfilled.

When you realize you are not just one amongst the many and start to grasp that you are an individual with an evolving purpose and destiny, then you won't have to be two halves of the same person. You won't have to strive to make up another persona in order to gain the acceptance of those around you. In fact, if you want to be authentic and unique, you will have to learn how to see the world for yourself and discover what role will give you satisfaction and peace. If you really give it some thought, we live in a society where manipulation is expected, and even admired on some level. Most of the people we look up to as role models have achieved that status by "tricking" us into believing that we won't be liked or accepted if we don't follow their rules or try to be just like them. Take a look at the media, for instance.

There are billboards plastered with pictures of "perfect" people and ads telling us that all of the smart consumers are purchasing their product. We are made to think that if we don't follow everyone else's lead and conform to the norm, then we will be "left out." In other words, we are told how to feel and when to feel it, and if we don't play along, then we are given the title of "outcast" or "crazy."

But what if you were able to see that your voice, your opinion, and your ideas carry weight? What if you learned to not just think for yourself, but make those thoughts known, without fearing the consequences of doing so? The conformists thrive on ignorance and degradation. They are counting on the fact that you will jump on that proverbial bandwagon and live your whole life in a daze, always being fearful of self-awareness. They don't want you to wake up, because that would mean that they no longer have control over who you are, what you do, and what you choose to believe.

They don't want you to find out what's real and what's fiction, because then you would have the clarity that you need to break out of the mold and be your own authentic self. Clarity is what we all truly need if we ever hope to eliminate the hatred and obliviousness that are now ruling our world. It's what's required to end the racism that we still experience all across the globe, and to stop fearing others simply because they aren't like ourselves. Instead of believing what others have told you to believe, and doing what is expected of you, live your life without doubt, without ignorance, and without being afraid of what might happen if you let your real self-shine through.

Being yourself and seeking your own sort of happiness is to fight for your voice to be heard, and to know that some people just aren't going to like what you have to say or what you choose to do. What you have to remember is that their denial of you and your voice is their problem, not yours. If someone has an issue with the way you are leading your life, then that just means that you aren't part of the herd anymore and that you are being your own unique person.

Most people just cannot handle the pressure that comes from this realization. They don't want to put in the time or effort that's required, so they choose to be just like everybody else. It's easier that way, right? But it's not the way to be joyful or lead a life of abundance. If you are part of a group of people who cannot stand on a fundamental level with you, who don't believe in the values you hold dear, then you can give up on finding contentment. Ultimately, we should all be striving to achieve clarity of purpose in our daily lives. I like to call this the **CLEAR 5 EXPERIENCE**, and it's an integral part of the overall plan to become your best self. CLEAR is an acronym for:

Clarify roadblocks

Learn required skills

Embrace challenges

Amplify faith

Regain power to believe

Living your life based upon the CLEAR 5 Experience will enable you to achieve your goals, your dreams, and your own version of success, rather than leading your life based upon the boundaries that have been set by everyone else. You deserve to live your life

passionately every day, and will only be able to do this if you are
ready to seek out who you truly are, embark upon your own path,
and never settle for the status quo.

The Power of Finding Oneself from Research to Revelation

"The idea of who you are must never be a borrowed one."
– *Dilshad Dayani*

As we read about gender perspectives and how success is perceived and aspired to as a goal in life by women and men, we see how attributing meaning to our busy, mechanical lives is extremely important. Would we dare to come up with something different or similar?

This book will help you put the notes and lyrics in place so you can hear your own melody singing in your heart. The problem most of us experience when trying to better understand ourselves is the thought of what we might uncover. After all, regardless of what you might find while reflecting, you have to live with yourself for the rest of your life. What if you reveal something about your own inner self that is shocking or that totally obliterates any preconceived notions you had of yourself?

Psychological studies have actually shown that a majority

of us find it difficult to be honest with ourselves about our skills and our overall performance in various aspects of life. We all claim that we are better at doing certain tasks, or that we are more likely to succeed when compared to others. In fact, a psychologist at the Australian National University, Dr. Cordelia Fine, has termed this the "vain brain" phenomenon. According to Dr. Fine, humans go to great lengths in order to deflect blame and set ourselves above others, thanks to our egos (Fine 2005).

This fear of what we might find if we take the time to reflect upon our own lives is also what drives us to seek out distractions. We busy ourselves by watching TV and listening to music. The next time you are out in public, notice how many people just cannot bear to be alone. They will either appear in pairs or groups, or if they are alone, they will distract themselves by talking on the phone or surfing the web on their tablets or phones. A quiet mind or silence within ourselves is one of the most frightening aspects in today's fast-paced sound and image governed world.

How to Overcome Fear of Self-Discovery

White Noise Escape:
In order to understand yourself and to go from simply acknowledging who you are to loving how you evolve, you need

to escape from the white noise that is all around you. You'll need to spend some quiet time with yourself and learn how to assess your thoughts and feelings so that you can learn from them and grow as a person. You see, the painful feeling arises not when others don't understand you, but when we fail to understand ourselves. The greatest hurt comes from our own inability to grasp who we truly are. We have to be open to listening and give ourselves an opportunity to hear and understand our passive voice, which is deep within our core. This can give us the power to unveil the most secret treasures about ourselves, breaking the shackles of all our limitations.

This can help us to shed the self-pity, the fear of experimentation or trying, and the unhealthy self-esteem that we've developed over the years. It can also enable us to rise above it all and take us to the enlightening moment of self-discovery that is blessed to us within our DNA.

Practicing moments of listening to oneself is essential. In those quiet moments, your goal should not just be hearing what you have to say, but also truly reflecting upon your liberated self that was once caged by conformity. Give yourself the permission to live in the moment, to be alone without feeling lonely, and to dive into your emotions, spiritual being, and inner thoughts without guilt or hesitation.

Try Meeting Yourself in Nature:

Have you sat alone with yourself lately, free of any distractions, and thought about how your day went or how you handled different situations? Do you recall having some quiet time, when you could delve into your thoughts and emotions without feeling guilty about taking some time away from your family or friends? We are all social creatures, to varying degrees. Mothers especially are conditioned by societal norms to be givers only, and so they are often discouraged to take time off for personal rejuvenation; if they do, they feel guilty. If we take time out of our day to be away from our children, then we are looked down upon by others, or we feel as though we are neglecting our duties. However, this couldn't be further from the truth. It is only in these precious moments we set aside for ourselves that we can better understand who we are, confront our weaknesses, appreciate our strengths and recharge our core to deliver our tasks.

How you transform from the experience of solitude and develop valuable attributes determines and identifies your worthiness.

I look forward for your new revelation!

Practical Tips:

- A great way to achieve this freedom is by journaling or meditating. Take time to sit down each day (write it down in your schedule if you need to), and even if it's just for the time being, let go of all the worries and stresses you've been holding onto.

- Do your best to focus on the moment you are now in, and don't allow anything to prevent you from reflecting upon your feelings and ideas.

- Think of this time as an opportunity to just be yourself and find out what you're all about.

If each of us gave ourselves this gift, the world would be a much better place. We would be proud to be who we were born to be, without doubt, shame, or fear of suppressing our inner voice to arrive at our calling.

Your gender must not put a limit on how you inscribe your success, nor should it dictate how you decide to arrive at your checkpoint. It is only the mind that can drive your potential to imagine, give you the power to seize every opportunity and freedom to create your own version of success.

Chapter 3

How Culture Embeds the Idea of Success

"The first step toward success is taken when you refuse to be a captive of the environment in which you first find yourself."

–Mark Caine

Take a look at these statements made by people from different regions of the world:

I cannot marry someone outside the family or continue my studies, as it is against our tradition and the family honor.

–An 18-year-old female from Afghanistan

I would have loved to go to school and get a degree and enjoy opportunities like other men, but untouchables are way behind in any progress and due to the cultural caste system, we are deprived of even basic human rights in our own country.

–A 21-year-old male from India Dalit community

Does demanding equal pay get you fired because you are a female?

In May 2014, Jill Abramson was fired from her position as the executive editor at The New York Times. According to Ken Auletta at The New Yorker, several weeks prior to her abrupt termination, Jill Abramson and her lawyer made a "polite" inquiry with Times management about why her compensation and pension benefits were markedly less than Bill Keller's, her male predecessor. "She confronted the top brass," one close associate said, "and this may have fed into the management's narrative that she was 'pushy,' a characterization that, for many, has an inescapably gendered aspect" (Auletta 2014).

Jill Abramson's story is a perfect example of how cultural ideals influence the notion of how much success can be stretched, particularly for specific genders in certain contexts. It's interesting how structures, policies, and mindsets determine the way women draw parameters of their success. The space they share in the corporate world is challenging, and talent and expertise are not given their due share.

A study conducted in 2012 by Pew Research found that the percentage of women who are their family's primary income earners had gone up. What's amazing about this isn't the study itself, but rather, the reaction some members of our society had when hearing about the findings. On a popular television network, Fox Business, an all-male panel commented that the results of this particular study were a sign society was collapsing. Others said women weren't supposed to be the primary breadwinners, as that was the man's job. They also went on to say men who weren't the primary income earners in their households weren't man enough (Mirkinson 2013).

These comments really shocked me, especially because they originated in the United States. I could understand how South Asians maintain their cultural code by pleasing their social circles more than their own selves, but not in America. The pressure to keep up with the Joneses drives many people to act contrarily in relation to the pursuit of happiness.

One of the roadblocks we encounter in my South Asian culture is academic pressure. In determining children's success, notions of material wealth and power are instilled and then attributed to certain professions. If that isn't enough, we discuss personalities and friends who have accumulated wealth and so-called status to validate how secure their life will be financially. Later on, the child who followed the cultural stereotype of taking parental advice often end up feeling miserable, as the idea that success leads to happiness begins to consume his or her life.

Many cultures validate a man's contribution as the ultimate definition of success for a woman. However, based on the aforementioned premise, how can a marriage as an institution be capable of giving a woman the respect and security she deserves as a human being? And does society even calculate the value of the human capital a woman contributes by building effective members of society when she raises her children to adulthood?

A woman's chores and responsibilities are always unaccounted for, whether she cooks meals, cleans, or supports the husband or partner. In this way, she also contributes to her male counterpart's success professionally by taking care of the home for him—if he is fed and dressed, and his basic needs are met, then he can focus on work. The emotional wellbeing he derives contributes to his physical energy and work performance, which are influential factors in his overall success.

This domain of parenting, the one of a homemaker, has never made headlines despite it being an important element for societal success. However, we are quite driven by the powerful and glamorous corporate world, and in addition to media messages, society reinforces the idea that working outside the home is the only way to define success.

In fact, the most frequent question a woman is asked is: do you work? This question has a hidden connotation of: are you employed? The implication is that taking care of one's children, maintaining a clean household, and ensuring that the family is well nourished do not constitute jobs or work in the literal sense. That has developed an unspoken but universally understood societal rule that having a "job" and "working" equals stepping outside the house and earning a salary, and this rule is so pervasive that gradually, women themselves have begun to believe this to be true. While some cultures think a woman and her family can only be successful and peaceful if she stays at home and raises a family full-time, others might say she is only successful if she is earning a six-figure income in addition to raising a family.

This made me realize how deeply culture embeds the idea of success into our minds. The media provides us with images of expensively dressed business people, saying that this is what we should live up to. The more money you have, the better, because money and your countless assets are the hallmark for success. And you can't truly be happy in life unless you always try to overachieve and own more than your neighbor. But the truth is that you will only find happiness and fulfillment if you are ready and willing to create your own version of a value map that has the stamp of your own handpicked cultural values and traditions.

Stereotypes are born due to our limited information and the way our minds process data and form concepts. In the present age and time, information is powerful, but "Googled" information is not always accurate, and this can lead to distortions in perspectives. The consequences can lead to wrong personal and societal decisions. Stereotypes, clichés, pop culture messages and sometimes even our circle of influence can unconsciously be a threat to our own pursuit of happiness.

One major disadvantage of these stereotypes we tend to overlook is the differences that make us unique. We begin to assume facts about people that aren't necessarily true. We make generalizations or simplify a person so much that they lose their individuality. In many ways, using stereotypes allows us to make the world easier to understand by cognitively reducing the amount of thinking and processing our minds have to carry out, especially when we meet someone new. When we stereotype, we simply assume a person encompasses a wide range of attributes and characteristics that all members of his or her group possess. But this leads to social categorization and even discrimination, which is one of the main reasons people develop prejudiced attitudes. It's the "us versus them" way of thinking.

Culture shifts drastically when people have strong beliefs or ideologies. Today, in the Western world, that belief is called capitalism. The almighty dollar is king. But capitalism stretches beyond economics and impacts our entire culture. In our capitalistic modern society, tech-centric mass media outlets sell us everything, even our ideas. They do it to meet the ever growing demands of cultural views that align with conformity and standardization. The individual, in many respects, is fading into the masses. It's important to understand that capitalism is not just an "economic theory" governing America's business world, but an ideology that goes against human nature. Having wealth and material things is not a biological necessity, and humans are not simply "machines" here to achieve monetary gain, as capitalistic ideals may suggest.

A quite fascinating example of how capitalistic societies standardized human beings and encouraged conformity can be found in an etiquette book published in 1889 called *Success in Society*. It was very popular in its day, as it helped immigrants and other members of the society determine what behavior was acceptable and what was frowned upon. The leaders of our society thought these types of books would be a great way to keep the working class civilized, and the population saw them as a tool to assist them climb up the rungs of the social ladder. This excerpt caught my eye, as it perfectly illustrates the concept of conformity in capitalistic cultures: "Never look behind you in the street, or behave in any way so as to attract attention. Do not talk or laugh loudly out of doors, or swing your arms as you walk. If you should happen to meet someone you know, take care not to utter their names loudly" (Fore 1990).

This is a historical example that exemplifies how we came to adopt certain behaviors and develop habits—sometimes good and sometimes without thinking—because we are used to following and not questioning. Even today, the etiquette manuals we rely on (i.e. magazines and television) instruct us on how we should act, how we should speak, and how we should dress in public. They tell what we should do in order to be successful, even going so far as to suggest how to raise our children and live our lives day to day.

Things really began to change for American society, in terms of conformity and capitalism, when the way we communicate transformed. Because of the surge in production within our country, and the way those goods were distributed and consumed communications evolved.

Before this time, all news was delivered through the town crier or locally amongst friends and family members. The news was a more personal thing, not something dispensed from an anonymous agency or writer. Friends from out of town would visit and tell you their experiences about a place, rather than a book or newspaper giving you its impression of a particular locale or event. Slowly but surely, we all became passive observers of the news, rather than active participants, listeners, or storytellers.

Then, in the 1950s, news was transformed into something more exciting and controversial. It couldn't be the plain truth anymore, and so it became an exaggerated or dramatized version of events because that is what the people wanted. They wanted to be excited and amazed by events, and the news sources gladly accommodated this need by mass-producing news on a grand scale, more quickly than ever before, even if it wasn't accurate or meaningful.

Radio, and then eventually television, changed our methods of communication and in turn our society as a whole. Capitalism spread as our communications grew. Encouraged by manufacturers, we began to consume more and more, and we were told that thinking like everybody else was the way to go. It was all about immediate gratification, spending extravagantly, and never asking why society became this way.

When I first came to this country, I found it difficult to describe what my heart really wanted and aspired to be. I didn't grasp why money was so powerful coming from a meager middle-class family or why it provided such emotional stability, because for me, growing up in my neighborhood I saw people who were poor and living in cramped quarters with large families, but who were still happy and secure.

When I decided to stay at home to work and take care of my child eighteen years ago rather than take a job outside the home, it was frowned upon by almost everyone I knew in the States. They wondered how I could waste my Master's degree in education and my multilingual skills.

However, it was important for me at the time to dictate my real worth. This book will help you reveal and confront the layers that mask beliefs, values, and inner aspirations. The messages in our culture saturate our minds with ideas that seem powerful and contagious, but quite often manipulate the masses to become part of the consumerist culture that is heavily dependent on buying habits.

As you reflect, you begin to realize you are running with the rest of the pack; you try to figure out whether this definition of success—the one that's derived from culture and capitalism—is even part of your meaningful equation.

Ask yourself:

Do I feel as though I can have it all without losing something valuable in my life?

Balance without Guilt: Does It Really Exist?

"I believe that being successful means having a balance of success stories across the many areas of your life. You can't truly be considered successful in your business life if your home life is in shambles."
–Zig Ziglar

How many times have you felt overwhelmed by the sheer amount of things happening in your life and the challenges you encounter at work and with your family? Do you feel guilty because you're unable to be everything for everyone?

At one point or another, we have all found it difficult to achieve balance in our lives. We become remorseful and start to feel as though we will never be able to achieve success in every aspect of our lives. This leaves many people wondering if balance is even possible, given the present structure of our economy and the requirements we have to fulfill in keeping up appearances in our lives. Are we always doomed to feel as though we are letting someone else or ourselves down in our pursuit of success? Does balance without guilt even exist? The answer to this all-important question is YES! However, it takes a great deal of mindfulness and self-awareness to achieve a fulfilling yet guilt-free life. A 2013 survey conducted by Hay Group, a global management consulting firm, found that only 39 percent of employees say they have achieved a work-life balance. The study involved more than five million participants who worked in more than four hundred companies in sixty-five countries. The research found that people believed their companies expect them to do increasingly more for increasingly less (Royal 2013).

This means that more than half of us are unhappy about the balance we have achieved in life. We feel guilty about being away from our families while we make a living, and then we feel guiltier at home because we believe we may not be making the most of our professional opportunities. It's a vicious cycle in which we constantly feel we are disappointing someone, even ourselves, or not living up to our true potential.

Here are some techniques that have worked for me in the past and have made a big difference in regards to how I feel about my own definition of success:

There are things you can control and those you cannot. One of the things that lead to guilt is feeling as though you have control over everything. You'll become overwhelmed and stressed, because you cannot wear all of those hats at once without something falling through the cracks. It's all right if you don't have control over everything. However, we live in a society where being in control of all aspects of our lives is expected, and that's asking for stress. We must learn to believe in the power to let go and be okay with that choice.

Understand that "me-time" benefits everybody. When you take time out to regroup and refresh your mind, everyone in your life benefits. Even though you may feel guilty about not spending the hour with your children or not devoting an extra evening to work assignments, being alone and unwinding from the day gives you an opportunity to become a better individual- wife, husband, mother, father, employee, and friend.

Don't be afraid to outsource. You can't do everything yourself. So, why not try to delegate tasks to others? You don't have to fit a million things into a small span of time just because you want to do everything on your own. Instead, rely upon your support system to help you out every now and then. I know, the world we live in sees asking for help as a weakness. After all, admitting we can't do it all on our own is a sign we aren't a superhero and we aren't cut out for an illusionary success, particularly those things that aren't a high priority.

Get your priorities straight. Have a clear sense of your priorities. What is most important to you right now and what can be let go? You see, we only have a finite amount of energy and time. You have to work on sorting out your priorities seriously to figure out your life choices. For example, you have to go to your daughter's recital, but you've already committed to meeting a long-time client. Decide what is most important to you.

Do you want to show your daughter your support by attending her recital, or are you more concerned about how your client would feel if you cancel? Would you risk losing your client and potential much-needed money by going to the recital? If so, is there a way to cut back on other things so that you can attend to your child if you feel the recital is a priority? This hypothetical scenario aptly shows how critical thinking and planning come to rescue you in the most comforting way and help you address the priorities you deem most important. Avoid being pulled in a thousand different directions, some of them unnecessarily.

Avoid multitasking as much as you can...be in the moment.

This one is going to make you think twice, and that's just another bit of evidence proving we are all affected by our culture, which has turned humans into circus performers. Hear me clearly! You don't need to multitask all the time to prove you live in the present or that you are **normal**. Multitasking has been ingrained into each of us to the point of addiction. We are taught that in order to be successful, we have to be able to do a number of things at once. We must answer phones, reply to emails, and eat, all at the same time or else we won't get the job done efficiently.

I am here to tell you that you will get enough done, deeply feel joy, achieve more balance, and enjoy the pleasure of being alive if you learn how to live in the moment and do one thing at a time. Work on crossing things off of your to-do list one at a time, so you can focus on the task at hand. Even though multitasking might be considered a great trait to have in an employee, it will do absolutely nothing for your life balance.

Consider all aspects of your well-being when seeking balance. You cannot be happy or be successful if you don't take care of your body, your mind, and your spirit. Your emotional health must also be pampered. When you try this, you may experience some difficulties in breaking away from certain habits. Remember that your idea of balance is dictated by your being able to take moderate amounts of all the areas you deem as priorities, and this has nothing to do with others' interpretations of how you should live your life.

Cultural Conditioning Can Create Road Blocks

"I don't know the key to success,
but the key to failure is trying to please everybody."
–Bill Cosby

How we are raised, cultural ideals and societal norms all play a major part in how much we try to accomplish—even our ability to achieve success. It can create roadblocks that inhibit our ability to focus on our true potential and find fulfillment in our lives. It is always a good idea to take pride in your culture and to learn from the experiences you have gathered. However, it can become a problem when societal or cultural ideas or traditions begin to violate your rights as a human being or hinder your pursuit of personal success. Nothing should ever stand in the way of you being your best and true self, not even the beliefs any culture has instilled in you over the years.

For example, if you have grown up in a culture that believes it is a social stigma for men to stay at home and raise children, then this may impact how you want to live your life as a woman. Your criteria to live in abundance may be to raise a healthy happy family with your husband's support and involvement, and create a harmonious environment. As such, even if you wanted to be a stay-at home-mom or switch roles or perhaps work part-time and create an unconventional value map, the deep-rooted culturally conditioned beliefs may constantly offend you. Therefore, you wouldn't find the happiness or fulfillment in life, because you have given cultural norms power over your present thinking, and in many ways, perhaps permitted roadblocks for your future.

Cultural conditioning has one of the most significant impacts upon your critical thinking abilities. If you aren't exposed to other cultures or are told your viewpoints are the only ones that matter, then questioning may create conflict. If other ideas come up that aren't in line with your current beliefs, even if they are more conducive to your own success and happiness, you will push them aside.

A study conducted by Duke University looked into how appearance, cultural conditioning, and success were associated. It was determined that CEOs who looked more competent made more money and were deemed more successful. A competent look was defined as someone who had rugged male facial features and looked more mature.

Another study conducted shortly thereafter found that African-American CEOs were perceived as more successful if they were clean cut and had a "baby face" appearance. During this study, participants were shown headshots of forty African-American men, white men, and white women who happened to be CEOs of Fortune 500 companies at one time or another. The participants were then asked questions about their perceptions of the individuals in the photos, such as how much they made and how competent they appeared.

Overwhelmingly, the participants felt that the African-American males with clean-shaven, rounder faces were more successful, competent and friendly. Surprisingly, the African-American CEOs actually did earn more (Graham et al. 2011).

However, the most notable thing about this research was that the participants allowed people's appearances to dictate their perceptions of how successful they were based on societal stereotypes, media messages, and what has been absorbed from cultural notes passed down from one generation to another.

The definition of competency and the notion of a successful image are so culturally embedded into our minds that it's hard to escape them.

"You were born with wings, why prefer to crawl through life?"
— Rumi

In order to remove the cultural block or conditioning predicament, you will use **CLEAR 5** as tools to overcome these obstacles.

Clear Roadblocks

If cultural ideals are holding you back, then let them go, get informed about new ideas or opinions, and transform your perception. It is ideas that nurture, not specific cultural brands.

Learn Skills to Address Day-to-Day Decision Making

Learn to embrace the skills such as objective analysis and unbiased judgment calling. These abilities will give you a healthy mental attitude toward oneself with a renewed perspective on life, thereby giving yourself the chance to experiment new boundaries.

Embrace Challenges

Understand and reflect your current definition of happiness. If you recognize how you presently view success, you can take steps to change the definition. This premise of self-evaluation allows you to create your own script.

Amplify Faith

Understand why you fail and ask if everything has to be as planned. If you believe in any God and practice any faith, there are certainly ways to attribute failures when you have tried your best. Faith in yourself and in any higher order will give you the power to be resilient, confident, and persistent with emotional security and of course peace.

Regain Power

Create your own value structure. Just because there is a belief in place (such as "women shouldn't enter into the work place demanding equality"), it doesn't mean that it's set in stone. Be prepared to get rid of the beliefs that hinder your progress and start changing your mindset.

I want to leave you with some important questions to ask yourself. All of these questions are designed to help you reflect and develop your personal definition of fulfillment and how you measure it:

- Do I know for certain that those I truly love feel loved?
- What are some of the things that give me true joy?

- Have I paid attention to my blessings and expressed my gratitude?
- Have I made someone feel better today and did I avoid using words that might have had the opposite effect?

If you want to be your best self in every way imaginable, then you must be willing to set aside harmful cultural norms and build your pyramid of success. I want to share something that was adapted from a story by Dr. Edward Prather that really drove this point home for me:

A wise man lived in an African village situated next to a lake. He happened to know every secret of life. On one particular day, two village children decided to put the wise man's knowledge to the test. They asked him, "What is the secret to success?"

Without uttering a word, the wise man took each of the children's hands and walked them over to the lake, then into the warm water. He did this until they were completely immersed, with their heads covered by the water. Neither child knew how to swim, so they started to panic. However, just before they ran out of air, the wise man brought them out of the water and back onto the shore.

The children panted for breath and screamed at the wise man, "Are you out of your mind? We could have died!"

The wise man replied, "Right before I pulled you out of the water, what was the most important thing to you at that very moment?"

"We just wanted to breathe!"

"Exactly," the wise man said before walking away. "When you want something in life as much as you want to breathe, then you know you've found the secret to success."

The story is brilliant because it tells us we will find success when we find something that drives us, which makes us passionate about life. We all have the power within to be happy and successful, but most of us aren't willing to take the time or make the sacrifices required to achieve it. If you observe every culture on earth, without exception, there are standards and rules in place.

These rules must be followed by every member of that culture who wants to fit in and achieve success, which is measured by that societal group. Ask yourself the question: how do you define your own culture map of happiness and success? To what extent can you analyze, modify, and craft your own meaningful value-based map to construct your unique place in the grand scheme of things.

How far are you willing to travel to find yourself?
"I want to sing like the birds sing, not worrying about who hears or what they think." — *Rumi*

Chapter 4

From the Principle of Deficiency to Efficiency

"Our deepest fear is not that we are inadequate. Our deepest fear is that we are powerful beyond measure. It is our light, not our darkness, that most frightens us."
–Marianne Williamson

I n the previous chapter, we confronted roadblock three—how our brains get wired with cultural messages that are not created by us. We either become victims of indisputable ideas from childhood or allow them to become security blankets, until we realize they are senseless or are in conflict with the peace in our lives. We continue to collect perceptions in the form of traditions and assume that if we forgo customs, the guilt will be merciless or we will be cut off from the social circle that feeds these behaviors. Remember, conformity feeds comfort zones and help us sustain our emotional safety nets.

Later, we begin to follow a value system that pollutes our

life and makes us miserable. We have not been taught how to engage in an ongoing filtering process or how to take a different route and therefore, we don't encourage our children also to think outside of the box. Even if a custom or tradition wastes time and energy, and it does not contribute positively to our lives, we won't even think of getting rid of it. This is because that custom has become ingrained.

The fourth roadblock to happiness and fulfillment is what we call culturally imposed inadequacy. We allow the world to dictate our limitations and what we can or cannot achieve—all based upon ideals of what is accepted and what is taboo. The hardest-hit segment of society, which is more than half of our world population, is often treated as a second-class citizen.

As you may have guessed, I am talking about women— people who are rallying through yet another civil movement to empower their children and themselves.

Many of us have grown used to the unfair metrics in place designed for women, and our job is to simply follow those social standards, pick a set of norms, and attach to a specific group for life. When I came to America, many of my friends told me I would face stereotyping at work or even discrimination, but I experienced something different.

I never paid attention to what I was not able to achieve, and instead focused on achieving that which was difficult. We have to start breaking the molds that people and culture create for us.

In my South Asian culture, very specific ideas about the roles of men and women and their capabilities are present. However, this is true for every society. Women are often deprived of their rights due to cultural myths and traditions that handicap their ability to act rationally as a human being. They start to develop a platform of deficiency, and that becomes their premise. Every woman, to some extent, has compromised in one way or another by adhering to unfair societal norms, even in developed countries like the United States. An example of this is inequality in salaries and work schedules. These seemingly common sense but in actuality discriminatory societal norms add to an already unfortunate situation for women, and they also show how many of these inequitable measures against women are tied to economic and financial statuses, such as salaries.

- How do we prevent gender stereotypes so women will have a voice, too? How do women fulfill their true purpose and avoid falling into the mile-wide gender gap that has evolved over time?

- Who dictates these terms, and why are we still adhering to preconceived notions of pleasing, getting approval, and marriage-derived success?

- What factors are really involved in the success of men and women?

- How do these values have the power to change the course of our lives?

- And how, exactly, does one's gender lead to feelings of inadequacy?

Certain studies suggest that the personal definition of success is slowly but surely evolving. The bad news is that our culture is full of gender barriers and clearly defined, archaic gender roles.

The Gender Gap and Inadequacy

"Women have been taught that, for us, the earth is flat, and that if we venture out, we will fall off the edge."
--Andrea Dworkin

The gender gap is a societal condition based on the premise of inadequacy. As children, we are taught that gender determines what we can do with our lives, rather than our abilities. For example, a phenomenon across the world is that girls grow up, get married, have children and devote their lives to raising a family. And even if they work, they are still the primary caregiver and the secondary income provider. Often, even when women make more money than men, they still do most of the work at home.

These are the cultural norms implanted in our minds from the moment we are old enough to comprehend the basic rules of life. Generally, girls are taught early to compromise, confine, and cage their capacities to suit male-dominated societies. They are told that women who are more assertive aren't likely to get married and will end up scaring away potential suitors.

Rather than intelligence and self-sufficiency being key traits for development, women are advised that these things eventually lead to loneliness and unhappiness. Interestingly, commonly discussed on talk shows is the way in which women are having a difficult time finding their significant other.

What we must examine, in order to prevent this from happening all over again in the future, is the question of whether or not these norms are changing for the next generation. The way I see it, they are changing, but the pace is very slow. However, women still have a great deal of pressure, especially those who feel they have to prove themselves. Take a look at the plight of single mothers. They have to do it all with no support system from society. They have to find childcare and affordable health care for their families, and oftentimes they have no work flexibility and are given the standard number of paid leaves as all other employees. Responsibility weighs heavily on their shoulders.

In turn, all of these factors make women less aggressive in working environments. They feel complacency will provide them with job security, even though they don't earn as much as men. After all, their families are depending on them. They are afraid to negotiate and are perceived as intimidating if they try to fight for better wages, even though they know they are worth more. Women accept lower starting salaries and often end up doing the same or more work for less money. They put a lower price tag on their self-worth out of necessity.

Research conducted in 2012 studied the correlation between gender gap beliefs and how they influence our ability to perform in life. One of the most popular theories is that men perform better than women in science and math. The study, which was conducted by a University of Illinois at Urbana-Champaign researcher, involved 144 children, ages four to seven years old. The participants were asked to play a game with 3-D blocks, which were displayed at different angles.

Then they had to match pairs of images that appeared at varying perspectives. After one round of the game, a moderator of the study told one group of participants that the other gender group was "good at this game." Another group was told that a particular participant was good at the game. For example, they may have been told that the girl sitting next to them was excelling. A third group was told nothing at all (Cimpian et al. 2012).

Then the children were asked to play a second round, which was more challenging. The scores of participants who were told that the other gender was performing well fell by 12.8 percent on average. The scores of the children who were told about another individual doing well stayed roughly the same, while the scores of those who were told nothing fell by 2.9 percent.

Even though a total stranger told them that the other gender was good at that particular game, they still absorbed the information and took it at face value. It had a direct impact on their performance, because they were told the other gender was better at the task (Cimpian et al. 2012).

These findings suggest that we indeed internalize cultural beliefs that relate to our abilities. In other words, when women hear "girls aren't good at math" often enough, it becomes true to them, because they gradually accept it and give up on excelling in that subject. It becomes part of our belief system and we, as women, begin to identify with the idea that, because we are women, we cannot be good at math or science.

We force ourselves into a state of inadequacy, because that is what we hear around us. We start to associate a particular image our gender should portray in order to be appreciated and become objects of approval. Gradually, we start believing our identity is somewhat lesser, and in doing so we experience peace and less conflict with the other gender. In essence, we are limited by what we should be, rather than striving to find out who we can be.

This is a tragedy. Imagine how many people have failed to find their passion or fulfill their life's purpose, simply because they were told it wasn't possible. The issue that underlies inadequacy is how we define capacities and faith in each gender.

The model nurtures male-dominated systems while expecting females to bend and compromise - a total conflict with a human rights perspective. Instead of the system changing and evolving, women are still expected to negotiate their happiness by fulfilling family obligations in the name of respect, honor, and societal structure, in order to work around it without questioning—even if that entails long-term damages.

Factors that promote the principle of inadequacy and inefficiency in women

"Men are taught to apologize for their weaknesses, women for their strengths."
–Lois Wyse

In a 2013 study conducted by Citi and LinkedIn, a rather notable discovery was made that I think says it all when it comes to how we view gender roles today. When asked, men tended to describe themselves as being "confident, ambitious, and family-oriented," while women were more likely to say they were "good listeners, loyal, collaborative, detail-oriented, and happy" (Drexler 2013).

Typically, there are straightforward values that drive both genders. For example, men tend to believe they should be in control and stronger. They are told from a young age that they should be powerful and assertive, and tackle issues immediately, rather than thinking it over at length before taking action.

On the other hand, women are generally told they should be more emotionally driven and focus on being kind. This nice connotation subtly suggests women to "let things go." They are led to believe they can ask questions, dwell over a particular task or issue, and then move forward. In other words, women are thinkers and men are doers. These are the core values and attributes each gender is supposed to possess if they want to achieve success.

Gender-based roles today seek desired attributes and values instilled at birth to prevent the breakdown of the familial structure. The problem with this theory is that it limits us in every possible way. It prevents us from doing what we want with our lives, and it uses fear against us. At the other end of the spectrum are those who never do what they want with their lives because they are unaware of their inner strength and power. They don't know they can achieve greatness and do amazing things, because they have bought into gender barriers or cultural myths and norms. Challenging these gender-based values is often easier said than done.

It can be difficult to balance cultural values with what we want to achieve or accomplish in our lives. For example, certain families in South Asian culture often look to one family or community member to take care of the extended family or someone who is sick. Gradually, they expect that person to be around all the time, and consequently take his generosity for granted.

These caretakers, with unending expectations set forth for them, go through an inner conflict of personal guilt versus ethics. A part of them may not wish to upset the balance, while another part knows they can achieve their own success if they could just say that this is not fair and break free from tradition. As such, the situation escalates into inner conflict and personal struggle. We must learn how to break through the boundaries created by gender roles, while staying true to our core beliefs.

Breaking the cultural code and arriving at something significantly meaningful and powerful to you will require a trade-off of your comfort zone—at least in the short run. This is a simple example of confronting and navigating your inner core fundamentals.

Breaking Through the Glass Ceiling

*"To tell a woman everything she may not
do is to tell her what she can do."*
–Spanish Proverb

I've heard the term "glass ceiling" often in recent years. Though it's usually used in the context of our professional lives, I think it applies to every aspect of life. It is this glass ceiling that prevents women or certain cultural groups from achieving success. It is the invisible barrier formed by society's norms and the values instilled within us all.

A report released in early 2014 by Catalyst entitled, *Women CEOs of the Fortune 1000*, took a close look at female CEOs and their level of success. The study found that women CEOs who attain high positions often discover they have less power than their male counterparts. Additionally, only about 4.5 percent of the CEOs of Fortune 1000 companies are female (Catalyst 2014).

The study involved information from several different databases, including the 2011 *Financial Times* list of the top 50 women in business. For the purpose of the study, the researchers took an in-depth look at CEO duality, wherein which a CEO is also given the board chair title within the company. This duality has served as an indicator of how much power a particular company has given to a specific individual. When viewing this information, the researchers discovered there weren't many differences, demographically, between male and female CEOs.

Despite this fact, female CEOs were more often given the title of CEO/company president, rather than CEO/board chair. The interesting thing about this is that the title of company president typically holds much less power than that of board chair. As such, women who worked hard to achieve the level of CEO in their companies were still, according to the study, not usually given the same amount of power as male CEOs.

The researchers summarized, "The research suggests that female CEOs, even when their leadership is as effective as men's, have the additional challenge of earning legitimacy in organizations that favor and reward stereotypical masculine values and practices. In other words, women have to work harder than men to prove their worth."

While this study pertained to a business aspect, it speaks volumes about gender roles, feelings of inadequacy and the gender inequality that still exists within our society. Just because a person is female, it does not mean she should live her life governed by antiquated concepts of what a woman "should be." The same goes for men, for that matter.

I want to leave you with a story that I think perfectly illustrates the idea of gender inadequacy, the glass ceiling, and gender barriers created by culture. It's not my personal story, but one a family member shared some years back, and it has always stuck with me.

There was a woman who grew up in a home where being a woman meant that you were demure, quiet, and subdued. She wasn't taught that she could be and do anything with her life, but that there was an important role each of us was born to play, and hers was to be a wife and mother one day. She grew up, got married at the age of twenty, and then had two daughters.

The woman was dependent. She relied on her husband for everything and dreaded the thought of being alone. When her children were at school, she would spend her days keeping house, always sure to have dinner ready by the time her husband returned home from work. She supervised homework and tended to her children's needs, and it went on like this for years. She never thought to get a job, because that wasn't part of her family tradition. She didn't get a driver's license, because she was told that, "since your mother didn't have a driver's license, you shouldn't be able to drive either."

In every way imaginable, this woman was ruled by what others had told her over the years. She lived her life based upon the cultural identity created by society and relayed to her by her parents. And, while she had a family and a husband who provided for her, she wasn't happy. She wasn't satisfied with the way her life had turned out, even though she had followed all of the rules.

One day, after her children had grown and left the house to make lives for themselves, her oldest daughter came to visit for coffee. It was their weekly custom. Her daughter would bring a dessert to share, and they would chat for an hour or two, before the daughter had to leave for work.

You see, even though the mother had taught her daughters the same ideals she'd been taught—women belonged in the home raising children—the oldest daughter had other plans in mind. She knew she wanted to do something different with her life, and that she wouldn't be happy or satisfied if she followed in her mother's footsteps.

The daughter had known for quite some time that her mother was unhappy with the path she'd taken. She realized her mother had sacrificed a great deal for her family, and had many talents she never explored because of it. So when they sat down on this particular day to chat, she asked her mother why she'd done it.

"Why didn't you ever try to do something different with your life? I appreciate you doing so much for us, of course. But what made you want to give everything else up?" Her curiosity had finally gotten the better of her, and she just had to know the reasons behind her mother's decisions.

The mother thought about this for a moment, before giving her daughter an answer. "This is what was expected of me. There are times when I do have qualms about not doing something else though, not that I regret having you or your sister for even a moment. But there are times when the regret is heavier than usual, and during those times I envy you a bit— especially the fact that you didn't listen to all of my nonsense about having to be one thing or another, because you actually became that rare sort of person who is able to live her life free of the limits others have created for her."

For years, the daughter had looked at her mother with pity and mild disdain, because she thought that she was weak. But now she saw the truth. Her mother was afraid of defying convention and not playing the part she was supposed to play.

The daughter fully understood that her mother's belief that she was inadequate and unable to be something more was what had held her back. She realized the only difference between her and her mother was her ability to question convention. After all, if it doesn't make sense, then you should leave it. Rules, norms, and traditions are followed to bring happiness, comfort, and peace to individuals and families. The daughter refused the path she was led to and created her own version of happiness, leading to success. This was reflective of contextual factors instead of the success her gender dictated for her.

The story clearly indicates there is absolutely nothing wrong with women wanting to raise children or men wanting to be the providers. However, there is a problem if the person following these gender rules doesn't want to play the role or wishes for more flexibility rather than abiding by rigid norms.

If people live their lives in a constant state of inadequacy, rather than empowering themselves to live the life they have in mind, then that is the real tragedy.

In the next chapter, we start the journey of how we can change and leave behind some of the less valuable elements we have adopted from the experiences of others—the traditions and culture. Now we know what dominates our thinking and agenda for life, what creates structure, and how often we are compelled to follow traditions or norms so that we are not frowned upon.

But the question to ask is: if it does not make you happy or add value to your life, and if it fails to align with your own inner harmony, is that ritual, custom, belief, or practice any good?

Your cultural roadmap must not contain any vague elements. It must help you identify ways to achieve balance for meaningful success toward an authentic and fulfilled purpose, and an extraordinary self within you.

"It is not only the most difficult thing to know oneself, but the most inconvenient one, too."
– H.W. Shaw

Chapter 5

From Comfort Zone to Adventure Zone

"Life begins at the end of your comfort zone."
– Neale Donald Walsch

I n the last four chapters, we confronted the ideas, beliefs, and the foundation of our thinking agenda. We explored why we think, what we think about, what forms the basis of our value paradigm, and what forces are responsible for the cultural map that we choose to lay out; our experiences shape our perceptions and influence us. Challenging and questioning our cultural values help us to see our place in the universe with clarity and conviction, without having to conform blindly to norms and practices.

We discussed how culture, perceptions, beliefs, and traditions develop our social ability and help us to interact with one another without watching our words and actions at every turn. It is significant to keep in mind that culture teaches us the nuances to operate within society, and often we are unaware of the influence it has in our lives. Though culture is necessary, it also has the power to hinder our behavior and thoughts.

In the following milestones of our journey, you will see how we overcome the rest of the roadblocks to face our behavioral patterns. We will grasp the practical tools needed to craft a culture of our own. We will see what it takes to shape our ideologies within the context of our family, dreams, hopes, and the ultimate legacy we aspire to leave behind.

Now, we all could belong to the same faith and yet have a subculture of our own. There is nothing wrong with that. You may wish to become whomever you want, choose to wear what you like, and raise your children based on a conservative or a liberal philosophy. The important premise to establish is your limitless potential and your belief in yourself. It is crucial that you first plan to move beyond the group approval cliché. This is a courageous step down the path of rediscovering yourself.

When you read something inspiring, such as a motivating quote, you may perceive a wall standing in the way. Interestingly, there is a reason behind this phenomenon. Science explains the challenge of moving away from your comfort zone and offers an explanation for why the wall can be good for you. I have also been terrified by the notion of executing something new, fearing what it would demand of me. How much time, money, patience and courage would I have to invest to execute this new idea? No doubt, much more of each than I was expecting to give.

Simply put, your comfort zone is a pattern of behavior that becomes a set routine meant to minimize stress. The benefits of this are obvious: happiness, lowered anxiety, and relaxation. It is certainly safer to stay in our own bubble of predictable outcomes. As I confessed earlier, some of my uncomfortable zones were simply the product of my circumstances and cultural conditioning. Growing up, I often felt uncomfortable about my unconventional spirit of dreaming big, as I challenged beliefs and norms. I can now say that looking back, those inner conflicts created inhibitions that prevented me from unfolding my wings and flying fearlessly. Instead, I let my fears restrict me beyond the outskirts of my self-imposed boundaries.

As we hear about oppression and restrictions regarding gender development, many of us have observed that many young girls go through similar feelings and later accept it as fate or destiny to create a secure bubble. They face oppression or gender restrictions, like birds that are caged and seem sad at first, but after some time they adapt because they have no other choice. The oppressed girls end up fighting in a system where regulations are placed but not activated. However, many struggle to break the shackles while others succumb. This is a very pathetic scenario in our world and we must advocate rights for our children regardless of gender in order to help them achieve their full potential. The problem with leading our lives within the predictable comfort zone is that it doesn't allow us to achieve 100% of our potential. To see ourselves bloom with our full potential we must be willing and able to travel past these lines we've drawn for ourselves and see what lies in the "adventure zone." *How do we do it?* Let's ask these questions to reach our clarity zone first: How do we allow ourselves to break through fear and limitations so that we are able to take the risks that come our way? How can we be our true selves if fear is holding us back? What happens once we break through the barriers?

There was an experiment involving mice conducted in 1908 by Robert M. Yerkes and John D. Dodson. The researchers found that when the mice were under a reasonable amount of stress or anxiety, they actually performed better. However, once they passed the state of "optimal anxiety," their performance levels significantly decreased. The researchers concluded that we are more productive when we aren't in our comfort zones and are experiencing a bit of stress, but too much discomfort hinders productivity. Therefore, we must balance our lives somewhere in between (Yerkes and Dodson 1908).

The key is finding your comfort zone. Everyone's is

different, you see. Fear is the number one thing that keeps us from venturing out of our zone, and it is also what makes our zone grow smaller. If we are afraid of our economic future, fear for our families in times of war, or experience any other dreads and concerns, we become less likely to step away from safety to explore the beauty of the unknown.

Feeling Powerless: Health Scare 101.

"What we actually learn, from any given set of circumstances, determines whether we become increasingly powerless or more powerful."
-Blaine Lee

I have a great friend who is the perfect example of someone who was stuck in her comfort zone. She had a daily routine she followed to the letter. I watched her pass up opportunity after opportunity, all because she was afraid of trying something new. She was terrified of what it might bring into her calm and settled life. But one day, something happened that transformed her perspective—she got sick.

My friend experienced a health scare. She went in for an annual medical exam thinking everything would go as it always did: blood work, weight check, a conversation with the doctor, and a clean bill of health. She expected favorable results and would then go about her life, business as usual. However, things did not go according to plan.

She got her blood work back and it showed strong signs of cancer, and later it was confirmed. Her doctor told her if she had any chance of being healthy again, she would need an operation and possible treatments afterwards. Now she realized how this one thing she'd always taken for granted, her health, was jeopardized, and this experience changed my friend's perception forever.

Many of you reading this book might be able to relate to this example because a family member or someone you know has gone through a similar situation. I like to call this a perception makeover, because it changes the way we look at ourselves, the world, and what values matter to us most.

I witnessed a noticeable change in how she lived her life. She had been forced to venture out of her comfort zone in order to deal with her illness and to get better. Circumstance had provided her with a reminder of just how precious and fleeting life truly is. When we spoke, I could tell how much she had changed. Before her diagnosis, she didn't have the power to grow and learn more about herself. Now she was no longer afraid of the unknown, after realizing every day spent in comfort was one less day available to experience the true excitement, self-realization and new discoveries life had to offer.

Many of us have gone through something similar, where we have felt like the sky was falling or we were facing an insurmountable challenge. However, we were later surprised to know it was not as scary as we thought it would be!

Why does it take a health scare or something dramatic to make some of us see the truth? Why do we feel powerless before we are forced to venture any risks that lead to something truly amazing? So what is the biggest roadblock in trading a comfort zone for an adventure zone?

Fear is the catalyst for change!

"Nobody can go back and start a new beginning, but anyone can start today and make a new ending."
– Maria Robinson

When many people think of the word change, fear automatically begins to rise within them. The idea of venturing beyond the familiar terrifies them, because they simply don't know what lies ahead. What if taking a step toward something adventurous leads to problems? What if we cannot achieve what we set out to do? What if the change we seek ends up being for the worse?

These are questions we ask when we are about to step into something that is foreign to us. We begin to second-guess our decision and let fear push us back into the safe monotony. Society and cultural ideals teach us that we should trust things that are established. We've been told that if something has existed for a long time, then it must be true. We associate tradition with validity, and venturing away from tradition incites a painful fear in our mind.

The November 2010 edition of *Journal of Experimental Social Psychology* featured a number of studies about our fear of change that revealed some surprising findings:

- One study involved students who were shown course descriptions that had been used for quite some time, and then were shown a new description. The students preferred the original, even if it meant more coursework was involved. The researchers also found students liked a century-old description, rather than one written a decade ago.

- A group was given a piece of European chocolate and was told that the makers had been selling chocolates for seventy-three years and the same chocolates had only been around for three years. The participants stated the chocolates that had been in existence for seventy-three years had a better taste, even though in actuality, it was the same chocolate.

Ran Zilca, a writer for *Psychology Today*, released an article in late 2011, which stated, "We live in a society where comfort has become a value and a life goal. But comfort reduces our motivation for introducing important transformations in our lives. Sadly, being comfortable often prohibits us from chasing our dreams."

In our society, we have been taught to fear change. Why?

Questioning is challenging authority or conventional norms. Culture is a collection of learned behavior patterns; therefore, it is traditional and acceptable to follow the entire group in order to maintain conformity and peace.

We have been taught that longevity of any practice is to be valued, because people have been doing it for so many years, and stepping into the adventure zone would veer us away from tradition and practices that deliver comfort zone and help us maintain in some cases sanctity of those groups.

When we begin to experience fear, we shouldn't look at it as a sign that we are doing something wrong, but that we are doing something new and possibly transformational. When our body begins to respond to a situation by fearing it, especially if there is no basis for it, it means we're headed down the right path, and this fear is a normal phase.

It proves we are about to embark into a territory that will allows us to discover new things about ourselves and the world, so that we can truly derive the best out of that context and grow from it. Now, I know this can be easier said than done. After all, many of us have been conditioned to "color inside the lines" and stay on the beaten path. As such, we have to make a concerted effort to explore life and opportunities and confront them without the ties that have bound us to conventionality and cultural norms.

A report released in October of 2013 found that participating in new activities can improve the brain's cognitive functions. The ASSOCIATION FOR PSYCHOLOGICAL SCIENCE study titled, "The Impact of Sustained Engagement on Cognitive Function in Older Adults: The Synapse Project," discovered that doing something that is not only mentally challenging, but also out of your comfort zone, can help to boost mind functions and memory as we age.

For example, there are some people who come from cultures in which dancing is not encouraged, but when these people try it out, they end up discovering that they have superb eye, hand, and body coordination, which gives them not only satisfaction, but also a new perception about themselves, adding to their self-esteem and joy.

What the Adventure Zone has to Offer.

Finally, breaking free and venturing off to explore ourselves leads to unique and amazing rewards. What we must always remember is that most of these rewards wouldn't have been attainable if we didn't have the courage or conviction to say farewell to obstacles and break through our barriers.

It's okay to make a fool of yourself every now and then

and to forget about what other people think of you. We are all so terrified of being judged, of being called crazy or weird, but just think about all the amazing people you have met in your life. Chances are, some of them were unconventional, loud or thought outside the box, made a difference, and led a life of freedom and fearlessness.

So don't be afraid of how others perceive you. Instead, focus on how you perceive yourself, and be the kind of admirable person you want to see yourself grow into.

Also, in order to travel into the adventure zone, you must also take a leap of faith without focusing always on the outcome. Do it just because it will allow you to elevate your value and precipitate your growth. When you do something new, there's always that element of fear, but that's a part of taking risks. Sometimes the rewards will come and other times experiencing something new will be its own reward.

The people who really thrive in life are those who enjoy the unknown. The world is filled with challenges and setbacks, as well as victories. Those who meet failure and opportunity with a mindset of living to the fullest feel the abundance and gratification that comes with having a relentless spirit. Wouldn't you like to feel the anticipation and thrill that you get when stepping away from the familiar? Try throwing away the predictable map and moving beyond self-imposed boundaries.

When I first came to America, I was entering into a country and a life full of unknown situations. I was aware I would have to create a new life for myself, meet new people and live within a culture that was completely foreign to me. In essence, this was just about as far out of my comfort zone as I had ever been. Think of your personal stories in life and perhaps, you may have also encountered those check points where your decisions made people frown at one point in time, just because you attempted to be different.

Our stories may have different details, but they all involve changing the mindset before life can offer changes in a concrete form. That is the beauty of the unknown. It allows us to find out more about ourselves and what we are capable of achieving, because we can no longer lean upon the familiar. We gain the power of vulnerability, and our sheer will and strength open ourselves up to new paths.

I've put together this **Comfort Zone Checklist** to help you venture into the transformational. It's based upon the **CLEAR 5 EXPERIENCE** concepts, which will enable you to gain mental focus, self-awareness, and mindfulness so that you can achieve meaningful success and fulfillment in your life:

___**Clarify roadblocks to celebrate** every step you take away from the familiar. Even if it seems insignificant at the time, just having the courage to venture into a new activity or phase in your life is worth commemorating.

___**Learn new skills** every day. Even if it's just a new recipe or taking a different route to work, these small variations give you the opportunity to venture away from your comfort zone little by little.

___**Embrace challenges to examine** every "what if" question that enters your mind, and explore the possibilities that it would bring. Far too often we shrug off the "what if" opportunities in life because they involve change. But imagine what might happen if you actually took action and acknowledged the feasibility of "what if" questions; you may witness surprisingly pleasant results in the form of happiness.

___ **Amplify faith to allow** yourself to let go of the idea of perfection and fearlessly believe in yourself without worrying about other people around you or what they would think about you. Instead, learn from your mistakes and stay away from those who try to put you down or judge you because you are trying something new.

_____ Regain power and take ownership of your decisions so you can realize and navigate your action plan that makes you happy. It could also happen that you wish to aspire within your ethics code may not be considered acceptable by your social circles. Don't let fears of the unfamiliar prevent you from embarking upon your own transformational journey.

Ran Zilca, a writer for *Psychology Today*, has noted that, "Comfort equals boring shortsightedness, and a belief that things cannot change. Your comfort zone is your home base, a safe place not to stay in, but to return to, after each exhausting and exhilarating expedition through the wilderness of life."

We get comfortable with the way things are in our lives and often lose motivation to do anything, let alone something new. However, when we discover that our life is stagnant, we begin to feel as though we have failed in some way. Though change scares us, watching life pass us by can be more terrifying. There are also those who have a comfort zone and prefer to be rather unconventional. For example, some people might be so used to stress and anxiety that those emotions are comfortable to them. In such cases, they may feel happiness when in their adventure zone. For these individuals, going outside their comfort zone allows them to experience the true beauty of change, but also leads them to breathe more emotionally stable lives as they constantly seek change.

Parents can lead by example and encourage their children to push through the barriers that hinder their progress. We can show our children that there is more to life than playing it safe all the time and encourage their adventurous spirit. For example, if they wish to pursue surfing, or show interest in hiking or sailing, don't dismiss their interests, and instead, encourage them. They have not yet developed firm and fixed social limitations and are ready to unleash their power of imagination into the world. Interestingly, the sheer act of watching them brings pure joy and excitement, and this speaks for itself the power behind any fearless pursuit.

Children are free, and their imagination knows no bounds, because as mentioned before, they have yet to come across societal barriers and form personal boundaries; therefore, their comfort zones are endless. That being said, as adults, what we have to ask ourselves is: are we treating our comfort zone as though it is a sanctuary to return to after going on adventures, or is it a place in which we dwell all the time and use it as a scapegoat to get out of trying new things?

Remember, challenge is not always about success, wealth, power and winning. It is also about finding a new meaning in life and unfolding our spirit of discovery and wonder. Evaluate and question your present state and what you would like to experience. Are you stuck in life because you are too afraid to test new waters and become an explorer of your own future? Or, are you ready to embark upon a journey that will lead you to undiscovered territories and amazing opportunities?

Move beyond the margins to experience the joys life holds for you. Do something beyond the comfortable routines!

Chapter 6

From Personal Criticism to Compassion

"You can search throughout the entire universe for someone who is more deserving of your love and affection than you are yourself, and that person is not to be found anywhere. You yourself, as much as anybody in the entire universe deserve your love and affection."

-Buddha

Being human comes with inherent flawed, imperfect and vulnerable traits. As such, we must be compassionate with ourselves and be aware that suffering and feelings of inadequacy are normal. We all go through this. Rather than telling yourself that you are alone in being imperfect, it's important to remember that this is simply not true. We should be able to filter media messages that glamorize perfection and fog perceptions with superficial and edited images of reality.

We should also keep in mind that our feelings and thoughts may be influenced by outside forces and therefore, should strive to understand the basics behind media literacy and the coded messages. Parenting, cultural norms, and our environment are all examples of these forces. We make a plethora of choices each day—what to eat, drink, or wear, who to spend time with, when to rest or sleep, and which values we embrace, commit to, and live by. We strive to live a value-driven life.

But being happy in the here and now may be more complicated when people fall for temptations, giving in to an immediate reward by indulging in a promise of short-term hedonistic pleasure that conflicts with personal values and goals. After all, we are works in progress, you and I—two steps forward and one step back. Self-transformation doesn't happen overnight, whether you are deliberately aware or not, consciously participating or not.

Most times, we make choices out of habit, and it takes a real commitment to live intentionally to change those habits. We know that self-conscious emotions drive most of us toward avoiding pain and pursuing pleasure, and these will influence the choices we make, the opinions we hold dear, the insights we gain through self-reflection, and the ideas we accept as worthy of believing. But what happens when you find yourself deviating from your values and caught up in the many temptations that sabotage your best intentions?

When this happens, should you beat yourself up or show

a little mercy? Based upon your experiences, wouldn't you agree that we as humans have an inherent tendency to focus more on our weaknesses than our strengths? We are self-critical by default, rather than reflecting on areas in which we truly shine and thrive. I vividly remember when I was in college, trying to master a challenging subject: statistics. I didn't just want to learn everything I could about statistics; I wanted to really dive in and gain a firm understanding of all of its many nuances, even though it wasn't my strong suit.

I soon realized that I couldn't bring myself to fall in love with the subject. By then, the teacher had discovered my struggles, so he pulled me aside and gave me a simple but priceless piece of advice: "If you want to excel at anything, it's not enough to fix your eye on weaknesses. You also need to leverage your strengths."

He shared a story in class about Albert Einstein failing a French exam. My teacher explained that, if Einstein had concentrated only on his language skills, he might never have transformed physics. He never would have discovered the many formulas and theories that changed the way we understand the world, because he would have been hung up on the fact that he didn't excel in French class.

If you are self-criticizing because your pants don't fit or you think you may have said the wrong thing at the wrong time, write down the self-critical words that pop into your head. Then ask yourself: would you ever say these words to a friend, or would any of your friends ever say them to you?

The hardest lesson to learn for many people who come from South Asia like me is to be less demanding of oneself and not to raise the bar higher and higher. Now, I don't mean to say that we must not strive for excellence or pursue better opportunities, because we should all aim to do our very best. However, we must also give ourselves the occasional breaks and pats on the back, or else we will exhaust our psyche and our body.

Our effort to nurture positive thoughts in our mind must be an intentional and conscious attempt. We must be willing to retreat positively or embrace graciously a mental hug every now and then to keep us emotionally healthy and strong. The first lesson in love is to appreciate ourselves before we can even begin to understand and empathize with others. The fountain needs water itself to quench the thirst of other people.

"Over the years, I've learned that a confident person doesn't concentrate or focus on their weaknesses - they maximize their strengths."
– Joyce Meyer

It is essential that we address our weaknesses from a different angle. You may be thinking, "Well, this isn't exactly a new story, is it?" However, how many times have we ignored this same old advice and gotten the same old results that brought us to the same old places in our lives?

Many of you might be culturally familiar with the South Asian diaspora, which has a tendency to socially stigmatize people who try to seek advice or solutions by discussing their feelings in order to get support. I am fully aware that there are conditioned patterns of thoughts in cultures that create these road blocks, making it difficult to discuss your true self. In these scenarios, one must not be consumed by meaningless pride; rather, one should understand that there is no shame, for example in going to a mental health expert to seek help. Those who inflate their egos and place false value on their pride instead of accepting reality and getting proper treatment will never get well, but only degenerate. The pretense and fake appearances that we often see in society prevent us from building a healthy and productive mindset through which we can objectively strategize and contribute positively toward our lives and within our families.

However, we must seek to choose and get feedback from people who are our closest circle of friends, family members or non-judgmental people who are good listeners. You can even take some assessments online designed to help discover your true strengths. Whatever method you choose, it's important to acknowledge areas where we may excel and learn how to use those strengths to our full advantage.

Though it may be easy enough to establish our weaknesses, it's a whole different story when it comes to determining how they are holding us back. You see, a weakness has the potential to become an obstacle whilst we are trying to develop our strengths, and therefore, it can prevent us from achieving our goals or create mentally challenging and pessimistic thoughts that could prove to be degenerating.

Let me share a true story that my friend Isabelle told me. It's about a woman whose parents were professors who strived for perfection. She graduated with honors, attended law school, and then continued on to devote her time to charity work, eventually achieving great professional success. Her human rights endeavors saved countless lives, and she received award after award.

However, she experienced an important shift in perspective when she had a near fatal car accident. Up until then, she had always pushed herself to be the best. If she was near the top of her class, she wondered why she wasn't number one. If she joined the basketball team, she would criticize herself for not being the one who scored the most points. And, when it came to human rights issues, she was angry and frustrated. After she endured the car wreck, it put everything into perspective. She realized she would have to turn that anger into action and not let cultural ideas of perfection dictate her life.

Compassion, especially self-compassion, is part of being human. We need to be cared for on a biological level, and we need to care for others. But it's not easy to feel love for ourselves. In our society, we are actually encouraged to criticize ourselves so that we can excel; but we are also taught to treat each other with civility and politeness. Why is that? Why must we not show ourselves the same gentleness we offer other people?

There was an interesting report released by Psychologists Nick Epley and David Dunning that concluded that people consistently overestimate the likelihood that they would act in generous or selfless ways. This doesn't just apply to generosity either. In fact, people completely miss the mark when it comes to judging their own strengths in a variety of everyday situations or tasks (Epley and Dunning 2000).

Generosity is important to many of us, and in my life, it has been a very significant component from a very young age. I think it has played a major role in my life. I tried to justify my role as a young girl, observing pain and injustice to children and women on a daily basis and often blaming myself. I have been able to accomplish a little more by working extra hard. However, there were many times when I was under the impression that I had helped others successfully, and would change my mind of the outcome later if I did not get the results I had expected.

Later I realized and made a conscious effort to understand the fact that rather than judging myself or being overly critical of the difference or effort I had made, I must treat it as a life experience. I decided self-doubt in a conscious and healthy way would give me the opportunity to assess the data I had gained, to show me why and what had held me back, and how those weaknesses could enhance my understanding of myself and contribute toward my overall performance at work and home. By accepting and acknowledging the weaknesses, I found the answers that allowed me to become more generous, to fine tune my strengths, and to confront and master the art of being kind to myself. Once upon a time, there was a music critic who was able to write very critical reviews about musicians, simply by thinking of them as complete strangers or even non-persons.

One day, a famous musician strongly objected to a review that she had written. The musician wrote a scathing letter to the publication for which she worked. To her embarrassment, her publication printed that letter. Now she knew what it was like to be on the receiving end of public criticism.

Not long after the music critic went through her encounter with criticism, she watched a performance of a singer who had a very unusual style. She was not a fan. She started to write a very negative review of this singer, but then she stopped and changed her approach. She did not lie and write a rave review for the singer. Instead, she wrote about who this singer could be. She wrote about her potential and how she could become an excellent singer. The singer thanked her for the review, and after some years, did in fact become the type of singer the critic described her to be in her review.

The best way to move from criticism to compassion is to develop a sense of caring self-awareness. I've put together this **compassion checklist** to help you to stop the self-criticism and embrace self-compassion. It's based upon the **CLEAR 5 EXPERIENCE** concept, which will enable you to gain clarity of purpose and thought and to achieve the success and fulfillment in your life that you've been dreaming of:

___Clearly define your strengths and be open, but not overly critical, about your weaknesses. Transform your approach to personal development and self-growth by being patient and honest about your limits and the resources you can access.

__Learn and assess social norms. Be brave and jump to what makes you feel fulfilled and, and don't devote your time or energy to searching for perfection in everything or comparing your traits.

__Embrace your uniqueness and understand that every weakness you overcome is an opportunity to learn and figure out something valuable within you. Never doubt or shame yourself because others think you are not successful at a certain point in your life.

__Avoid the "should haves" in life and rewire your priorities. This premise will help you define a new culture map of things you value and things you wish to say goodbye to, such as traditions, norms and priorities set by societal or parental conditioning. What your parents thought was right at a certain time in your life may not align with your happiness now.

__Reactivate the ideals that you assumed as unattainable. Discover, launch, and dare to be a doer regardless of the fear of losing the security in looking perfect.

Simple and Powerful Ways to Calm the Inner Critique

When you're struggling to make a change in your life, it's tempting to see your mistakes as evidence that there's something wrong with you. Like me, you might find that your inner critic's voice grows louder and louder.

According to the teachings of self-compassion taught by Kristen Neff, PhD, real change happens in the moment we consciously offer self-compassion for the internal critic and its need to whip us into compliance.

Negative self-talk is self-defeating, dominated by pessimism, shame, guilt, fear, anxiety, and isolation—hardly a resilient, happy, or resourceful state of mind to actualize your potential and go for your dreams. Self-criticism does not work well when you view yourself as the problem. The brain works on what data we feed its circuits. Self-critics often don't even try achieving their goals because the possibility of failure is unacceptable.

The brain kicks in and attacks—"I can't believe I gained those 5 pounds back... I should've aced that project"—thus the self-critical self-talk. Even more problematic is that self-critics have a hard time seeing themselves clearly and identifying needed areas of improvement, because they know that self-punishment will ensue if they admit the truth; therefore, they deny there's a problem or blame someone else. Furthermore, when we try to motivate ourselves with criticism, we stimulate a whole lot of cortisol and adrenaline, activating our flight-fight response— again, hardly the best way to inspire motivation toward self-improvement. The flight-or-fight response, designed to protect us and keep us safe, becomes a liability when the threat is coming from our own self-concepts. Increased stress demotivates us, and we try to self-soothe utilizing quick fixes to feel good.

How Compassion Motivates Positive Change

I've discovered that I usually can't change my behavior by simply resolving to do something with nothing but my will.

"Knowing what to do is not the same as being able to do it. If that were true, people would find it easier to stick to their goals and resist temptations".

– Christopher Germer

Willpower is not like a dam that can block the torrent of self-indulgence. It's more like a muscle, which tires easily. Beating yourself up often turns a minor setback into a major relapse. But we *can* overcome negative patterns one step at a time through healthier ways of relating to ourselves.

When we find ourselves in the cycle of negativity and out-of-control behaviors, we become the cause for our own pain and distress. Research supports this observation and shows us that you don't have to feel bad about yourself to make a change. Paradoxically, taking an accepting approach to personal failure can help you to be more motivated to improve yourself. As the spiritual sages across different eras have pointed out, everyone suffers and everyone struggles on the path to self-transformation.

New scientific research is giving this ancient wisdom credibility and showing that when it comes to making a change, self-compassion is our greatest source of strength, because it activates the mammalian care-giving system of tending/befriending in the brain, thereby releasing feel-good hormones such as oxytocin and opiates. Mammals respond to warm, soft touch and a soothing tone of voice. So **a great self-compassion technique is using physical gestures of affection**, such as putting your hand on your heart and saying words to yourself in a supportive, soothing tone, acknowledging the difficulties in your life as if you were speaking to a distressed child.

Self-compassionate people are more likely to take responsibility for past mistakes, while acknowledging them with greater emotional equanimity. Studies have shown that whether you're trying to lose weight, quit smoking, or start exercising regularly, accepting yourself where you are—and forgiving yourself for setbacks—helps you to engage in healthier behaviors that will support you to your success.

Self-compassion gives you the strength to take care of yourself, even when it's tempting to succumb to an old habit. Whether you want to change a negative behavior (like overeating or yelling at your kids) or commit to a positive one (like working out or meditating every day), *the best approach is to tempt your* **happiness by cultivating self-compassion** and tapping it into a transformative power, so that you can stick to your goals—and experience a more fulfilling and happy life. I encourage you to look at your past actions with compassion, and see how much you have grown.

In the next chapter, we will see how the power of seeking wisdom from within can lead to our soaring up and beyond…

Each step toward your worthy self is a success, and it will bring more and more inner harmony that is untouchable by circumstance or time.

Chapter 7

Seek Within to Soar Higher

"Your visions will become clear only when you can look into your own heart. Who looks outside, dreams; who looks inside, awakes."
—C.G. Jung

W e discussed how important compassion for ourselves is before we can reach out to others. Mercy and patience to accept ourselves with pride and gratitude form the fertile soil in which we sow the seeds of abundance for all.

The late Maya Angelou is one of my inspirations, and when I let my quiet mind embrace her thoughts, I see peace walk straight through the door. She once said, "I don't trust people who don't love themselves and tell me, 'I love you.' ... There is an African saying which is: Be careful when a naked person offers you a shirt."

How can we seek within to soar higher?

There are four steps you must follow to rise and understand the power of seeking within to soar high:

- Self-reflection as a lifestyle
- Element of faith or higher order
- Absence of white noise to redefine priorities
- Serenity plan

The thought of self-reflection and self-admiration frightens many of us. In fact, some of us go to great lengths to lose ourselves in the distractions of everyday life, so we don't end up alone with our critical minds and thoughts. I believe this is partly because we are terrified of what we might find, or not find, for that matter. What if we start digging, only to discover we really aren't happy with the life we've created or the level of self-awareness that we've developed? You see, many of us are trapped inside our own bodies and heads. We go through life on autopilot, and we become passive observers. We watch everything go by, hoping that one day there will be an opportunity for us to venture away from the sidelines and get a chance to make a difference in the world.

But what if we each took the time to delve into our own psyches? What if we each began the process of reflecting, so we could discover the power that has been waiting to be revealed?

Taking a moment for self-reflection has a dynamic and powerful influence on our day, and even has social implications. Self-reflection is the process of transforming ourselves and our society. Society is transformed, one person at a time. Through the willingness to be kind and mindful to ourselves and to one another, we can change the world. We live in a culture in which the words *kindness* and *love* seem irrelevant and long forgotten. Being courteous to one another also seems to be a thing of the past. It feels as though anger, aggression, and greed are becoming prevalent, but a number of recent events have opened our eyes to new and even more horrendous realities—from school shootings to horrific acts of assault and murder. This offers us the opportunity to ask ourselves: What kind of world are we building and creating? How are we treating ourselves, and how are we treating others? Are we really worthy? We are beginning to question the culture around us and look at the world with a new perspective.

Our minds and hearts are constantly at odds with one another. Our hearts explore the world with emotion, thanks to the intangible force it possesses, while our minds view things from a logical standpoint. Sometimes this conflict allows us to find our true selves; this is when our hearts win out over our minds, after we have debated about whether or not we should go beyond our interests. We gradually gain the ability to fully comprehend the difference between meaningful loss and financial loss.

From a very early age, my faith and my parent's actions taught me to make life better for those around me. Many of you have probably done the same thing and are aware of the feeling that arises when you put the needs of others above yourself and spend your life serving others. Our actions and emotions are the result of constant consultation between our inner self and outer skin.

If you really think about it, many of the decisions we make are based upon our hearts. Our hearts defy logic and convention. They have immense power, but this can lead to financial loss, in some cases. However, in order to experience lasting gratification, one has to rejoice in the practice of appreciating handpicked, value-based priorities, which cannot be defined on a materialistic scale. Socrates said it best when he stated that the unexamined life is not worth living, and virtually every experienced and wise person you encounter is bound to agree.

It's only natural that we seek out advice and validation from our friends and family members, as well as other outside influences such as co-workers, mentors, and even the internet. But experience has taught us that feedback from others is usually biased. Society's values, cultural norms, and other factors are influencing their guidance.

There may even be a personal agenda that the person has in mind, which might not be in our best interest. Listening to others can be valuable, but we also have to heed our own inner voice to unleash our own power of intuition. Unfortunately, listening to outside feedback can be addictive, and it gradually builds layer upon layer of resistance to our own unlimited reservoir of insight.

Regardless of our age, cultural background, or financial status, what matters most is how we answer this question:

How do we help ourselves create our own diverse cultural map where we are able to build a legacy that is valuable and meaningful?

These are several things we should keep in mind in order to truly reflect upon our lives on a daily basis:

• How do we address challenges at work and home, from dealing with conflicts to raising a healthy family with harmony and a true sense of purpose?
• How do we stay true to our core and character?
• Whose lives have we touched?
• Have we learned how to gain experience from our mistakes without dwelling on them?
• What have we done today that will help us to leave a legacy for our children?

Ultimately, you must do what you love doing and go to sleep tonight knowing that you accomplished something that has either bettered your life or those around you. You have to love those who love you in return, unconditionally, and never forget those who have been there to support and appreciate you. It's also important to never lose sight of where you have been, but do not let this become a roadblock for you by questioning the undesirable elements of cultural norms or societal traditions.

Remember that it's okay to be selfish sometimes, but being selfless is the essential step in creating a life of happiness and fulfillment.

Our value systems evolve as we grow and enter into different phases of our lives.
When we talk about seeking within to soar higher, it means getting on the road that helps us to understand ourselves significantly, and arriving at a state of awareness, serenity, and bliss while still meeting the challenges of work, family and purpose.

"I can teach anybody how to get what they want out of life.
The problem is that I can't find anybody
who can tell me what they want."
– Mark Twain

Element of Faith or Higher Order.

"Faith is taking the first step even when you don't see the whole staircase."

-Martin Luther King, Jr.

There may be times in life when we question why we must endure certain events, tragedies, or situations. We wonder why things have gone the way they have, and we don't think that we can carry on, for one reason or another. But it's during these moments that we must learn how to have faith in ourselves and believe that there is some underlying, invisible plan for us.

I know that not everyone is religious, but if you possess the ability to have faith in something or a higher order, you may be able to better cope with the worries that come your way, especially when everything seems out of control. Research has shown that having faith can allow you to lead a happier life, given that you will be better equipped to deal with everyday stresses. This is despite the fact that many people, when going through especially difficult times, tend to question their faith and waver in their conviction to God—which is a perspective that I understand and respect.

A 2008 report authored by Professor Andrew Clark (Paris School of Economics) and Dr. Orsolya Lelkes (European Centre for Social Welfare Policy and Research) revealed that people who have faith tend to lead happier, more fulfilled lives. The team gathered data from thousands of surveys that were sent in by Europeans who identified as either Protestant or Catholic (BBC 2008).

The study also showed that those who had faith had better attitudes about social and economic issues. "Our analysis suggested that religious people suffered less psychological harm from unemployment than the non-religious," stated Professor Clark. The same also could be said for divorce and other marital issues. Typically, those who had faith fared better mentally in times of stress or sorrow (BBC 2008).

Having faith in our lives can enable us to see that there is a method to the madness, as they say. It can allow us to see that there is a reason behind everything in life, and that each of the experiences we endure prepares us for what lies ahead. And for this very reason, it's important to believe in *something* in life. It's essential to understand that you aren't alone and that there is a purpose for why you are here and for everything that happens.

I have known many people in my life who have had no faith or belief in a higher order. In fact, there was one person who I worked with many years ago, who was void of any sense of faith. She was the kind of person who went about her life thinking everything happened at random, and that there was no order behind the chaos. So one day, I asked her why she didn't have faith in anything. She replied, "Because seeing is believing, and I have yet to see any Higher Being making my life better."

What do you say to that? That's when I realized the basis of any faith comes from the inside and not the outside. Whether we choose to have faith in our own power, or the power of a higher order, we must begin by accepting the fact that it can only be developed through self-awareness and positivity.

If we have no time to understand and engage in the self-awareness process and enjoy the power of mindfulness, we cannot hope to have faith in the steps that will take us where we want to go. Faith is internal, whether its existence is proved elsewhere or outside in the world. Seek within to soar higher is about how we discover our quiet voice and learn from the silent wisdom that is constantly poured into us. What we have to bear in mind is that it can only help us evolve when we learn how to look at our bodies and minds as vessels of inner grace, insightfulness, and humility.

There is a quote by Confucius that I'd like to share with you now. "By three methods we may learn wisdom: first, by reflection, which is noblest; second, by imitation, which is easiest; and third, by experience, which is the most bitter." This sums it up beautifully.

Block White Noise: Redefine Your Priorities.

"Sometimes things in life happen that allow us to understand our priorities very clearly. Ultimately you can see those as gifts."
-Mariska Hargitay

There was a woman whom I met shortly after coming to America; we'll call her Elizabeth. She and I were good friends, and she was someone I admired. She was self-assured, confident, and knew what she wanted in life. In fact, I'd venture to say that she was one of the most determined and self-aware people that I have known.

When we met for lunch one day, we somehow ended up on the subject of how she was raised. She told me about how she'd had a less than perfect childhood. There was abuse involved, and she didn't get along very well with either of her parents. When she had the opportunity to get out of the house, thanks to an offer of marriage from her high school sweetheart, she jumped at the chance.

She left home and eloped. Elizabeth had plans to go off to college, but that never panned out. Instead, she decided to become a homemaker, and devoted the next five years of her life to making sure her daughter and her husband were happy. In many ways, she became the person whom everybody turned to when they needed a shoulder to cry on or a hand to hold through tough times. This was her life. And to Elizabeth, every aspect of her life was happy. She never took the time to question whether or not she was satisfied with the way things had turned out for her. Instead, she filled every moment with "static". She surrounded herself with the white noise of life, so that she wouldn't have to engage in the thing that frightened her most: self-reflection to confront the depth of her own satisfaction and purpose.

Her priorities were completely askew. Rather than seeking within to soar high in terms of what was most important to her, such as health and personal fulfillment, she had filled herself with the agenda of being a complete doormat.

Had her neighbor's plants been watered, like she'd promised? Did she set aside enough time to do the laundry for her husband and daughter, even though she'd wanted to soak in the tub and relax for a while? Was everyone all right, or did she need to work a bit harder and a bit longer to please them? She was running around with too much white noise and was unable to hear her own self screaming for help from within.

Elizabeth told me after the fact, she realized just how trapped she was in a life that didn't feel like her own because those priorities weren't hers, or to be more precise, they were not balanced. She allowed the noise to fill her head for so many years that it eventually made her afraid to see herself for who she had truly become.

We remember to take care of everyone else, but fail to do so when it comes to our own health and wellbeing. So, the question is, what can we do to get our priorities straight? I would like to share some suggestions that have worked for me in the past:

Say goodbye to negative thoughts. Questioning our choices will help us decide what is important and what can be set aside in our lives, but first we will have to welcome the optimism so we can learn how to get our priorities straight.

Learn how to take a break. Many of us lead lives that involve lengthy to-do lists and are constantly in a rush to get everything done on time. What if we just took a break from the hustle and bustle of everyday life every now and then, in order to reflect and let our thoughts catch up with our ambitions? We have to learn how to take time out of our day to regroup and refresh our minds, so we can be happier and healthier. This is especially true for our mothers who are on constant guilt trips for not giving enough.

Write down what you do on a daily basis. Sit down and write down everything you do every day. Then, I'd like for you to cross off anything extra that doesn't really need to be done. You see, more often than not, we are busy but not truly productive.

Focus on the small things that bring meaning and dwell on it to feel the joy.

Not everything needs to be done right now. We live in a society where immediacy is king. If something doesn't get done now, then we're considered procrastinators. But this isn't the case. Not everything in life is urgent, so be bold enough to say no and muster up the courage to do what you love and what holds of greatest value.

Think about the people who matter the most. At the top of the list should be "MYSELF". Chances are, most of us wouldn't even think to mention ourselves when we're thinking about who matters most in our lives, but we should. If we are happy and well cared for, then everyone in our lives will benefit and grow with us.

Reflect upon what's really important in your life. Last, but certainly not least, think about what's really important in life. Think about the values that make you who you are, and determine whether those values are helping or harming your overall outlook and success. Define the culture of respect, love, harmony and family driven elements. Sit down and reflect upon the things that are important to your personal growth and happiness. Focus on them as an integral part of your life.

I've created this **introspection checklist** to help you gain insight so that you can have the power to soar. It's based upon the **CLEAR 5 EXPERIENCE**, which will enable you to gain clarity of purpose and thought.

___**Clarify roadblocks** to your self-esteem, self-image, and self-determination. Is there something that is keeping you from respecting and appreciating your own ideas and opinions? Do you doubt your worthiness?

___**Learn skills, such as self-reflection and listening.** Both of these activities rejuvenate the inner voice and strengthen it. This in turn helps you to become calculated in your approach to sensitive situations and gives you the courage to express truly. You develop patience amid chaos without losing sight of your selflessness. The process builds balance and guides you in achieving your value.

___**Embrace challenges** and understand that believing in yourself and taking action to validate your feelings and ideas (especially those that go against cultural norms) may be difficult at first. However, as we discussed earlier, the practice of confronting and conquering inhibitions takes time.

__**Amplify faith** in yourself and your capabilities, as well as in the Higher Order that sustains and thrives your spiritual energy.

__**Regain Power** by listening to your inner voice—the silent guide that quietly empowers you and builds your creativity so you can craft your path with clarity and confidence.

Exercise: A Serenity Plan to Maximize Your Energy.

"He who has health, has hope;
and he who has hope, has everything."
-Thomas Carlyle

I have developed a "serenity plan" that I use in my own life in order to restore balance and boost my energy levels. I am, after all, a wife, mother, and a professional woman. I've been able to rely upon this plan to get more out of my busy day and to maintain my sanity when times become more stressful. I practice Prana yoga and dance (also known as Pranayama yoga), which allows me to tap into my vital life force and regain the energy I need to lead my everyday life. Pranayama yoga is often referred to as "breathing yoga," because it requires practitioners to control their breathing patterns.

In many ways, Prana helps us to get in touch with our bodies and the flow of our thoughts. It can allow us to slow down the busy lives that we lead and to remember what is really important. Prana can enable you to reap a variety of rewards, including the ability to breathe more effectively.

Energy is not just good for your body; it's also good for your mind. A study conducted by the University of South Carolina in 2012 found that regular exercise sessions can boost energy reserves in your brain, which allow your mind to work more efficiently. The study was published in *The Journal of Applied Psychology*, and involved a group of mice.

The researchers divided the mice into two groups: one group was left in their cages all day, while the other was placed onto a small treadmill to work out for half an hour each day for eight weeks. At the end of the study, the mice that worked out regularly could exercise on the treadmill for 126 minutes before tiring, while the sedentary group could only exercise for around 74 minutes. However, that wasn't the most surprising evidence of the benefits of regular exercise. The researchers also found that the mice that worked out on a daily basis experienced a boost in mitochondrial development in their brains. Not only did the exercise trigger new mitochondrial cells, but it also helped the various brain cells to communicate with one another more efficiently, protecting against age-related diseases or memory issues (Reynolds 2011).

The head researcher, Dr. Mark Davis, stated that despite the fact that this study was conducted on mice, it was "reasonable to assume that the same process is carried out in human brains." He went on to say that a 30-minute jog daily would be the rough equivalent of the exercise that the mice performed for the purpose of the study (Reynolds 2011).

There is so much noise in the world today, and so much static that can distract us from self-reflection. However, if we learn to silence this noise and push that mute button, we can see what is really important in life. We can then tap into the amazing source of power within us.

Seeking within may not be the most easy task. In fact, it often involves a great deal of confrontation, strong focus, and internal struggle, particularly if we aren't currently leading a life that will help us to achieve happiness and fulfillment. But if we take the necessary steps, we can soar to heights that are beyond imagining.

To be able to find our true selves, we have to ask the right questions. If we begin to formulate clear and intelligent questions, we receive powerful and life-changing responses. So why not devote some time to learning how to ask the right questions, both for when you are seeking within and when you are speaking with others. The results of doing so may amaze you. What I mean by the "right" question is one that gives you the power to look at things from a panoramic perspective. We have to look at things from different angles, even if it is challenging. Self-reflection transforms our mindset and brings positivity into our lives. We aren't perfect, but if we are self-aware, we become stronger and more enlightened. There are hundreds of people who can vouch for the power of self-reflection, including myself—join us in this thoughtful act and try it out by learning how to strengthen self-reflection.

"It is necessary for a man to go away by himself to sit on a rock and ask, 'Who am I, where have I been, and where am I going?"
-Carl Sandburg

Chapter 8

From the Power of Visualization to Actualization

*"The tragedy of life is not death, but what
we let die inside of us while we live."*
– Norman Cousins

*We have come so far in our thought process just by engaging our
inner dialogue and self-reflection. Taking this cognitive approach
often creates a paradigm shift and compels many of us
to take action willingly.*

*However, if we have a strong strategy to bring the forces of the
universe to fruition, then our intentions can ignite realities.*

The question we should be asking now is: how can we transform our dreams and imaginations into realities? Let me begin by sharing with you a story that, in my eyes, demonstrates the notion of going from ideas in the mind to action in real time with a focused process easy to practice and share.

John Assaraf, as one of the featured experts in the film "The Secret," brings to light compelling stories and is considered to be one of the foremost experts in the science behind visualization. He has created visualization boards in the past and, as he was unpacking boxes after moving into his dream home in California, stumbled upon one of his old vision boards. This particular board held a variety of images, but one stood out from the rest.

It was a photograph of the home that he had just moved into. It was not a similar home, or one that reminded him of this home, but the very same house he had just purchased.

Several years back, he had been going through some magazines and had found a photograph of this specific house. He had cut the picture out and glued it to the vision board, imagining how wonderful it would be to have a house just like it and often focused on his dream.

It is this power of visualizing what you want in life that has the ability to transform you. If you set your sights on something and remove the mental doubts that hold you back, you gain the power to manifest anything you want in life.

The problem most of us encounter is that we fail to understand how powerful our imagination truly is. We deal with suffering, tragedy and challenges, which leads to unhappiness and disappointment. What if we could tap into the power of visualization and use it to create the amazing life that we deserve?

Crossing the dream-to-reality boundary.

"Vision is the art of seeing what is invisible to others."
– Jonathan Swift

When I was growing up, I was fortunate to have parents who were very encouraging. My mother in particular was one of my biggest sources of motivation. Despite, the fact that she grew up as an orphan and had a rough childhood, my mother had an enthusiasm that allowed her to always see life as though it were a rainbow. To this day, I cannot fathom how someone who endured the challenges she faced was able to be so optimistic, but my Mother had this priceless gift.

When I think about dreams, I don't think of them so much as *dreams*, but actions we take in order to pursue an idea that has been incubating while we sleep. In many respects, dreams are latent, like seeds. If we wish to see a plant, we need to water the seed and give it what it needs to grow. Similarly, for our wishes to be transformed into realities, we have to do something about it.

I confess that this is easier said than done. In fact, there were times in my life when I was not encouraged and felt as though my dreams were forever out of reach. However, there are times when you just have to fight back against the cultural norms. You have to tell yourself that you do, in all honesty, have the power to turn your imagination into reality. You have to be confident about your own ability to achieve success, even if others might disagree or doubt your capabilities, which create roadblocks for you.

My concept of dreams, in essence, revolves around how far you can push to be what you wish to be. There is a caveat to this; we must also acknowledge that a balance must exist. If we are married or have kids, we need to ensure that we aren't sacrificing or negotiating with our children's futures and our relationship with them in order to realize our dreams. Even though each of us holds an immense amount of power inside, there is a limit to what we can do. We must be ready perhaps to compromise materially every now and then, which could come in the form of socializing, or purchasing expensive gadgets or luxuries that we feel we deserve to possess at a certain point in time.

With that being said, if you truly want to achieve success and break through barriers, then you need to be able to perpetually visualize what you hope to accomplish. Not only do you have to think about it, but you must also feel the emotions that come with it. When we visualize something with the power of intensity and tie it to strong emotions, the repetition allows us to create new neural pathways. Believe it or not, by doing this, we are constantly reshaping the chemistry of our minds. The more we visualize, the easier it gets, and the more we achieve.

If you really give it some thought, it makes perfect sense that we can manifest what we emotionally visualize. The universe is a blend of protons and electrons that are all working together to form a perfect blend of harmony. I've had the opportunity to listen to many accounts from people who believe that the intelligence of the universe responds not only to our ideas, but also to what we feel. The universe answers and reacts to my dreams and passions, and consequently, will match and mirror my emotions. But to what extent is this true?

There is scientific proof that visualization works...
Two notable studies have been conducted in recent years that provide physical evidence of the effectiveness of mental visualization:

* A 2004 study reported by the US National Library of Medicine National Institutes of Health revealed the power of mental practices. A group of weightlifters participated in the study, which measured brain patterns. They were each asked to lift hundreds of pounds of weights, and then were asked to only imagine that they were lifting weights. In some instances, the

researchers discovered that the act of visualizing lifting weights was also effective as actually lifting the weights (LeVan 2009).

* In another study, Guang Yue, an exercise psychologist who works at the Cleveland Clinic Foundation in Ohio, studied participants who went to the gym, as well as those who only visualized working out. Throughout his research, he found that there was a 30% muscle mass increase in those who actually went to the gym. However, the participants who didn't go to the gym and only visualized working out also exhibited a 13.5% increase in muscle mass. These figures remained steady for three months after the mental training was concluded (LeVan 2009).

Now, please do not stop going to the gym and just visualize it, as some of us may find another opportunity to visualize our perfect laziness. This is true for me as for many of you who are reading! Let's get more out of our muscle mass and focus the power of visualization on hard to reach goals.

It's all about mind over matter. If you believe you can achieve something, if you visualize it happening with frequency and intensity with emotions behind it, then you will accomplish it!

How often doubts create roadblocks in our lives?

"Our doubts are traitors, and make us lose the good we oft might win, by fearing to attempt."
—William Shakespeare, *Measure for Measure*

The problems we experience when it comes to fulfilling our dreams occur when we begin to doubt ourselves. We start to expect that less success and more failure will drive our path and eventually see it as fate. What we have to realize is that our perception of life greatly depends upon how we see ourselves. Are we faithful to our own identity?

Imagination, at its core, is the ability to create a mental picture. It is the power to take things that do not yet exist and form an image of them in a way your mind can comprehend it. Everyone on this earth has the ability to imagine to some extent. However, some of us have developed and fine-tuned our ability to visualize more than others, and have learned how to use it toward success and happiness.

Just like any other invaluable tool, you must learn how to effectively wield it. Culture drives us in a certain direction, which can sometimes be good, because it acts as a motivational force in the form of group approvals. However, we must reflect and ask how much we want to go along with the flow. Also, how much do we want to create a flow others might follow, and perhaps gain knowledge from the road we have paved? In order to tap into the immense power of your imagination, I'd like for you to keep the following tips in mind:

- Forget about any of the limits you have placed upon yourself, and try to visualize and focus on one wish intently. See the impact this exercise has on your life.

- Understand that imagination is like a journey on which we travel the world, making everything possible. Now the next step is to experience the idea in concrete form.

- Accept that you have the talent to envision positive things happening in your life before they even come to fruition.

- Visualize the things you want to see happening in real life, and run scenes in your mind as though you have already achieved your goals and aspirations. For example, if you are hoping to get a job, imagine yourself walking into your new workplace in a brand new suit, your hands trembling with excitement.

- Many people start off by imagining what they can achieve—in other words, very feasible wishes, like getting a cat or going on a vacation. But expand your vision and think about the things that you truly *want* to achieve. Determine what you want to acquire, achieve, and become in your lifetime and envision it.

- If you see victory, success, health, abundance, joy, peace, and happiness, then that is what you can expect to receive.

- Visualization affects not only your thoughts, but also your emotions. Just having an image in mind will have absolutely no effect upon your life, but if your feelings are also invested, you can create a frequency, which in turn produces excitement, inspiration, passion, and eventually connection. This allows you to tap into the power of visualization to emotionally experience what can become a reality within your life.

True success, the type that transforms your life, is always created in the mind first. Regardless of whether you are striving for financial, social, physical, or relational success, it will only happen if you imagine it in advance. Add to that the power of emotion, and you provide the subconscious mind with the ability to transform mental images into reality.

The Key to Making Your Mental Movies Come to Life

How would you define your mental movie?
Is it action-driven or more melodramatic?

We all have mental movies we play in our heads; I like to call this "brain cinema". These are the day dreams we allow to take shape in our minds. We have to make sure that the outside world is a complete reflection of the world we have created inside. Visualization consists of imagining that you have achieved success, down to the smallest detail, so you can turn it into real life success. This is how you create the vibration that you are going to need to attract good things.

The key to making your mental movies come to life is to understand that you have to rewrite the script in each and every one of them, so you attract abundance and happiness. Set aside the antagonism and doubt; these don't have a place in your script. There is no room in your movie for negativity!

Some Easy Action Ideas to Practice

- Use a vision board to help you stay on track and maintain focus. I've used vision boards quite often in the past and continue to use them, because they are effective when it comes to keeping up that motivation and maintaining momentum. Include images that symbolize different things, such as a picture of a flower if you want to work on building your "blooming" self-confidence or picture of a moon to create "peaceful thoughts." It is like riding an imaginary horse that will take you where your aspirations are.

- Begin to create actual brain cinema. All you need to do is find free images on the internet. Google the names of the objects, people, scenery, and so on that you'd like pictures of, and copy and paste them into a word document. Once you've collected the images, type out what each picture symbolizes. Use the document you created to help remind you of everything you want and everything that means "success" in your eyes, and then visualize them on a daily basis to create your reality.

- In addition to visualizing, an emotional tie to your thought process is significant and a prerequisite to stir action in your agenda. Likewise, if you just sit around waiting for something to happen after you've visualized it, nothing will happen.

Emotions in our society are often labeled as "reactive" and are usually underestimated. However, emotions allow us to develop the power of fully immersed intent toward a particular goal. Without them, we may not be able to change our perception into reality, since emotion plays such a powerful role in changing the thought patterns and vibrational signals we emit into the universe. It sets everything in motion.

I've put together this **visualization checklist** to help you to transform your dreams and hopes into realities. It's based upon the **CLEAR 5 EXPERIENCE** concept, which will enable you to gain clarity of purpose and thought.

__**Clarify your thoughts** to develop the clarity of imagination. You need to clearly draw a picture in your mind of what you want in order to obtain it. Focus and refocus to get the right goal in your mind.

__**Let go of perceptions** and feelings that fog your emotions and block your thinking. Don't let them hold any power over you. Visualization can allow you to accomplish great things, only when you are working with the ideas that need to be materialized.

__**Embrace imagination** you must be prepared to embrace your imagination, and realize it's not just "make believe". It has the power to transform your life if you use it truly to serve your intentions with action plan drawn around it.

__**Amplify faith** by truly devoting yourself to sincerely accomplish your beliefs and ideas. The realization will fuel the process and give you the power to bring true realities to fruition.

__**Regain power** by manifesting your daily routine through reminders and personal notes. Stay on track and place your sincere faith in it. In order to persevere and be persistent, one has to find a comfortable act of discipline that works and gives results.

To end this section, I would like for you try an experiment, just to illustrate how powerful visualization can be.

- Imagine yourself standing at home, in front of your refrigerator. You reach for the door and open it. Now, I want you to grab the pie that's sitting on the second shelf. It's filled with ripe, spiced apples that have been baked to perfection, and the crust is a nice golden brown color.

- Take the pie over to the counter, take a knife from the drawer, then cut a big slice and put it onto a plate. Smell the cinnamon and look at the juices pouring from the sweet, baked apples inside the crust.

- Now, I want you to stop visualizing and pay attention to your current physical response. Chances are, your mouth is watering, and you have a sudden urge for a nice, big piece of pie, or even for just spiced apples.

You see, our minds can conjure images and thoughts that have a direct bearing upon the rest of our body. We tend to draw a line between that which is imagined and that which is real. However, it's not as cut and dry. Reality is not as tangible as we may think, just as imagination is not as frivolous. What we have to understand is, inventors and visionaries have been putting imagination to good use for centuries and have changed the world as we know it. In fact, there have been recent studies conducted in the field of neuroscience that have shown evidence that our imaginations are closely linked to our realities.

Try practicing if you are a mother to visualize your child as a positive and intelligent being in his area of ability. Log the results of this manifestation of comfort and impact and share with your friends.

And there are countless other areas where you can visibly see the power of imagination and perceptions. For example, the results of political elections are dictated by how a candidate was perceived, not who they truly are. Writers appeal to our imaginations in their works of fiction, drawing us into worlds of their own creation. This is because what we believe is far more powerful than what really is.

One of the most profound sentiments on this topic came from Buddha, Himself, who stated, "With our thoughts we make the world". Our thoughts are what change our lives and the world around us. Everything great or terrible that has ever happened on earth began with a single idea created by the imagination, and then transformed into a reality by emotion and action. There is research that suggests Tibetan Lamas have different brain chemistries, thanks to years of focused thought and meditation. In MRI scans, it was discovered that these lamas had strengthened brain centers, which is the area of the mind that deals with attention, compassion, and emotional balance.

Some thoughts laid out in this chapter may not be surprising, but one thing is intriguing—the majority of people in our society barely believe in these powerful practices. I assure you if you start this beautiful practice with your children or yourself, you will be astounded by what you gain. Also, do not forget the benefits you will receive through real-time in action, once you've visualized the life that you truly want.

*We all have the power to manifest what
we imagine and believe...*

*So long as we practice mindfulness to experience our
transformational being.*

Chapter 9

From Living Life to Leaving a Legacy

*"It is not what you do for your children,
but what you have taught them to do for themselves that will
make them successful human beings."*

—Ann Landers

Another big part of leading a life that isn't hindered by cultural norms and societal rules is leaving behind a legacy that allows the next generation to flourish and thrive.

*

While you may think your life is fulfilling and that you achieved success in your own right, you must ask yourself if what you are doing today is going to help those who will follow.

*

Will your life make an impact upon your children or the individuals who will inherit the world you've helped to shape?

Leave a Footprint Behind:
How Self-Awareness Leads to a Lasting Legacy

"Knowing yourself is the beginning of all wisdom."
−Aristotle

A uthor Ray Bradbury included a particularly poignant quote in one of his works that I think everyone should lead their life by. "Everyone must leave something behind..... Something your hand touched in some way so your soul has somewhere to go when you die....It doesn't matter what you do, so long as you change something from the way it was before and you touched it into something that's like you."

Simply put, you must be the change you want, and you must live life fully aware of the fact that you are leaving a legacy for those who follow. For example, Ray Bradbury said, "The difference between the man who just cuts lawns and a real gardener is in the touching. The lawn-cutter might just as well not have been there at all; but the gardener will be there a lifetime."

Ray Bradbury's words ring true. Our time on earth is short, and we must make it so that we last forever through our deeds that can transform and impact the next generation.

Unfortunately, many people do not understand that they aren't really living, but merely surviving. They are going through life with the fast-forward button firmly pressed, without realizing that they are wasting their God-given talents. Instead of waking up and discovering who they were meant to be, they are content with just being who everyone else expects them to be.

There is nothing more tragic than leading a fast-forward life, watching the moments go by in a blur without understanding yourself. There are those who are consumed by various gadgets, who are completely occupied by media and flashing screens instead of human interaction and conversation. Mesmerized by graphics and sounds that merely distract them and keep them entertained, but do nothing to add to their personality, character, or human qualities, these people are devaluating their latent potential.

We were born unique for a reason—so that we can contribute the best of our abilities, while always striving to be better. But how can you become your most authentic self if you don't even know who you are to begin with?

Sure, it is easier to live a life that is lived for you, instead of being an active participant. It's safer to sit in that crowd and watch the story unfold in front of you instead of jumping up on stage and joining the tale. However, that won't allow you to grow as a human being and do things in life the majority of people wouldn't dream of experiencing. To lead a life of purpose and to leave a legacy, we all have to keep one key thing in mind:

N*othing great has ever been achieved by just sitting back and letting life pass you by!*

Leading an Unscripted Life

"The purpose of life is to live it, to taste experienceto the utmost, to reach out eagerly and without fear for newer and richer experience."
—*Eleanor Roosevelt*

There are people who lead life by the book. They don't color outside the lines or veer away from the course that's been set for them. These individuals are leading a scripted life— a predetermined life dictated by societal norms. What if you could free yourself from this script to lead a fulfilling life, while setting an example for your children?

A major life lesson many of us overlook—and one that has the power to transform our mindset—is that our children have the ability to teach us just as much as we teach them. We often approach children as mentors, their guides through life.

However, it's often more likely that they are the ones giving us the perspective and insight we need to lead a life that is free of self-imposed limits. The young aren't burdened by preconceived notions. They don't know about the rules society has set for us, nor are they aware of the fact that we should act or live life a certain way. They are free of prejudice and cultural limitations. Every day is a new opportunity to explore the world with an open mind. As such, they offer us the gift of unburdened perspectives, curiosity, wonder, fearlessness, and a forgiving spirit.

When we learn to see children in this aspect, we have the power to change our lives and leave a lasting legacy. In return for this abundance and youthful wisdom, it is our duty to give them the emotional balance and enrichment they need. We must help them to develop compassion leading by example, and showing them that loving themselves and others can transform the world.

There are those of us who continue to do what the world expects and ignore the lessons our children teach us. They don't comprehend that youth possesses a certain naivety and innocence that is contagious if open to it. Instead of understanding that our children can show us how to be better people, they choose to believe the wisdom we collect with age is paramount.

The tragedy is that these people are secluding themselves from the beauty that happens when you become the student. When we open ourselves up to learning, amazing things come into our lives. Think, how afraid we are, to break away from binding traditions and conventionality, which often prevents us from making a change today for a fulfilled tomorrow.

Compassion Is the Most Powerful Gift

"If you want others to be happy, practice compassion.
If you want to be happy, practice compassion."

-Dalai Lama

Compassion is, without a doubt, the most powerful gift you can give your children. Without compassion for oneself and others, you cannot hope to have a rich life full of love and hope. In turn, your children will not realize their true purpose, or become beacons of light for those they meet along the way.

Compassion is the root of all religions, faiths, and beliefs. We have forgotten what it means to feel for someone else. In fact, sometimes it is even seen as a sign of weakness in capitalistic societies.

It's odd that kindness and consideration is now a strange or misunderstood concept, especially since the world is now more connected than ever. We have computers and mobile technologies to help us reach out to people across the globe, but we have lost the ability to reach out with our hearts and souls. Religions, more often than not, misinterpret teachings and perhaps judge others who are different than us or who don't comply with similar social norms.

Despite the fact that society and religion should be advocating compassion and understanding for a unified vision of a global community with all of us, we are often engaged in being critical of ourselves and of those around us. People are being denied their rights on a daily basis, and cultural "rules" stipulate that we should turn a blind eye to these people if they are different. If they think or feel otherwise, then they don't deserve our sympathy?

As Confucius so aptly said: "Do not do to others what you would not like them to do to you." And we should instill this value not only within our own minds and hearts, but those of our children. The primary ways to do this is to teach our children that our way is not the only way, that what society dictates is not always right, and that compassion is the way to self-awareness and self-enlightenment. Cultural beliefs and traditions would rather vouch that they know the true path to a successful and happy life, rather than accept that there are many paths that lead to a fulfilled life. Here are a few things I've learned along the way to help you develop a compassionate legacy and leave behind a world that is better than when we came into it:

- **Practice mind-ful compassion daily.** We must be mindful of compassion each and every day. It must become a part of our life style, rather than something we merely practice. If we do this, it becomes a habit and begins to shape our perceptions and thoughts. Begin your day by saying to yourself (and encouraging your child to the same): "I have the power to make a change and to show kindness and compassion to those I meet today".

- **Safety and security are necessary for compassion development.** According to Helen Weng, a compassion researcher who spoke at the 2012 compassion conference in Telluride, Colorado, there is evidence that suggests self-preservation typically wins out over compassion. If we don't feel safe, then we are less likely to feel for another person's needs. As such, it's important to make your children feel emotionally safe, so they are able to develop compassion and translate their feelings into best possibilities.

- **Relating to one another can facilitate compassion.** Instead of noticing the differences between you and someone else, notice the similarities. How is your life similar to their life? By teaching your children to do this, you are giving them the ability to relate to other human beings on some level, which builds compassion. They begin to think about how connected we all are, rather than focusing on the differences that put barriers between us.

- **Understand that you have the power to relieve suffering.** Teach your children that they have the power to help those who are suffering. Ask them to think about someone they recently encountered who may have been suffering in some way, and what they can do to help this person. Seeing suffering in real life is much different than just thinking about the idea of suffering. Giving your children the power to identify suffering and to think about ways to remedy it can be a life-changing experience for both you and them.

- **Do one kind thing every day.** Every day that you wake up and feel lucky to be alive, you should make a point to do at least one good thing for someone else. It may be something small, such as helping someone to cross the street or bring groceries to their car. Even these small things can make a difference in someone's life, and be a catalyst for them to develop compassion themselves.

- **Shedding new light on those who treat us poorly.** Sometimes the people who need the most kindness are those who mistreat us. When we have the ability to forgive these people and to look at them in a different light, we can begin to feel true compassion. For instance, if someone has unkind words for your child or makes them feel small, ask your child to think about why this individual may be acting this way. Could they be having trouble at home? Could they have an issue with their own self-esteem? Putting yourself in someone else's shoes and then being able to feel for this person is the key to unlocking empathy.

Research reported by Seeds of Compassion states that 80 percent of a child's brain is formed by the age of five, including emotional development. In fact, a vast majority of emotions emerge by the time that a child reaches thirty-six months of age. Concepts of contentment, joy, pride, and anger all form at an early age, making it essential to develop compassion as soon as possible. It's never too early to start teaching your child the strength to empower and make a difference.

The best way to transit from criticism is to develop a sense of caring and self-awareness so that you can build your legacy. I've put together the "**leaving a legacy" checklist** to help you stop the self-doubt and start making a difference for those who will follow in your footsteps. It is based upon the **CLEAR 5 Experience**, which we can use in every domain to re-energize our mental energy and channel it in the right direction.

This concept will enable you to gain clarity of purpose and thought, and to achieve the success and fulfillment in your life that you've been dreaming of, in order to pave the way for your children:

__**Clarify roadblocks** to your strengths and be open, but not overly critical, about your weaknesses. Transform your approach to personal development and self-growth so that you set an example for the next generation in a positive way and your children see you as positive influences.

__**Learn skills** and plan activities to help your children develop empathy, such as doing acts of random kindness and supporting those who strive for various causes. Engage them as leaders to carry the initiative and make it part of your value system and unique culture map. Help them to see things in a new light and to feel for those who are suffering.

_Embrace challenges by transforming your approach to everyday obstacles. Show your children they have the strength to overcome any hurdle. Display authentic behavior to thrive amid diversity and everyday challenges of work, family and purpose.

_Amplify faith to question the "should haves" in life so you can rewire priorities and be the change you want to see in the world and those around you. Focus their attention to live a simple yet fulfilled and abundant life respecting environment and people. Show them the value of people and humanity and steer them away from excessive materialism.

_Regain Power by translating your new skill set enjoying inner harmony through peaceful practices of mind, body and spirit and reaching out to those in need. Give your children the tools and guidance they need to empower themselves in order to find their innate purpose. Let their passion bring humanity closer and build their self-esteem so they can look back and feel the touch of your eternal sharing.

Here is a true story of how the parents of Emily, guided her to embrace an act of compassion and leave their footprint in the form of their teachings...

Emily James, a compassionate and spunky 3-year old girl, decided, with the help of her parents Amy and Richard James, to donate her long hair to kids who lost theirs due to illness. Emily's parents happen to be filmmakers and documented the process.

We suggested to Emily that we cut her hair off and donate her hair for wigs for cancer patients. We sat down and explained to her what cancer was, that some kids got really sick and lose all their hair, and that people can donate their hair to make wigs for these kids. We told her it had to be cut really short to get enough length from it and Emily told us she was excited to 'share her hair'...on the condition that "uncle Maffew would cut Dolly's hair too".

What Emily did, that was most meaningful to us...was that Emily was willing to give something that she had a lot of, something that could be of great meaning to another person. What we hope though, is that as Emily matures she will learn to make her own selfless decisions that inspire and bring hope, even if there is a cost.

To make the transition from long hair to short hair easier on the little girl, Emily's stylist first cut her doll's hair giving it the same chic bob that Emily would be getting. Then it was Emily's turn.

There is not one right way to raise a child or to leave behind a legacy that is meaningful and powerful. Each of us must find our own way to make a mark upon the world and the minds of those who follow. However, there is a common thread that weaves its way through the past and the lives that have made a difference in the world: compassion.

After spending some time learning and introspecting our experiences together, I would like to share what has captured my meaningful success. My successes revolved and evolved around my children. They were my highest priorities, and personal material gain was secondary. I was ready to simplify my wants, and even my needs to some extent, in order to be with my children when they were young. I did not want to indulge in any other material pursuits that could take away my energy to enjoy and be in the present moment with them. I thoroughly feel that I made the right choice, despite the fact that I was not seen as conventionally smart at that time because I gave up my earning potential outside the home.

However, as I have expressed repeatedly, it is vital to be self-confident and insightful in order to learn what is important rather than popular. We must be able to hear our inner calling and make the decision to see the big picture in our lives by first staying true to ourselves. We must also understand that marriage is an institution that needs growth, and we need to cultivate the precious relationships that are in our care. We cannot go very far without our spouses' support, and they too cannot be successful if we do not clarify our specific roles. It is very significant that in our relationships, we are insightful and stress clarity and productivity, in terms of energy and emotional worth, to get the ball rolling in the right direction. This requires tremendous patience to see our role and our personal calling.

I don't ever feel remorseful in regards to how I have pursued my goals within the nonprofit world, consultancy and spending time with my family. In serving others and completing the many required tasks, I learned how to manage my time, and I discovered how I truly wanted to spend it.

I cannot emphasize this enough, but this specific attitude was the deciding factor which enabled me to chase my aspirations in many domains and empower others. One of my most essential navigational tools has been listening to my intuition and paying attention to the learning potential in my mistakes because the litmus of experience is priceless.

I am aware of the fact that many of you have had the mind and humanitarian heart to grace this Earth and make a difference in your own unique ways. You all have two things in common— you feel for those around you, and you have made a conscious choice to put your compassion into action!

And today, I can say with confidence that you can surely teach the art to live and to love abundantly! Do not stop and continue to be the power of change that is within you…

Are you ready to spread the message of your innate passion and leave behind a legacy that speaks of compassion?

Conclusion

Abandoning Boundaries

*"The only limit to our realization of
tomorrow will be our doubts of today."*

-Franklin D. Roosevelt

s we take the last step in our journey, engaging thoughts
and emotions to experiences and challenges, the moment has
arrived for you to act. We learned to generate our metrics of the
value system that would help us define and not just conform our
unique culture map.

No doubt, it will require a significant investment of
conscious effort and time, because it is an intentional cognitive
exercise. A paradigm shift will help you to question and confront
the soft spots of cultural conditioning and comfort zones that can
be modified to achieve your worthiness and justify value.

I revealed how culture has the power to shape us and
how it influences what we can achieve. On one hand, it limits our

potential by making us feel that independent thoughts will make us outcasts, or impose gender-based restrictions and limitations. On the other hand, it helps us live together as a society, while we trade off skills and build harmonious communities.

There is nothing wrong with enjoying group approvals, activities, rituals, and being happy. However, the problem lies in how much conformity is acceptable to feed our emotional safety nets. When certain things conflict and interfere with your inner peace, remember to seek mindfulness and question the values around you.

I have attempted to help you reflect on the immense power you hold. The exercise is a habit of periodically re-evaluating our culture map, which is made up of choices. To conquer your doubts is a cognitive practice—an acquired habit learned by asking why a cultural norm should hold a place in your life and why it can't be challenged.

The ability to see through the guiding principles of life and embracing values true to your heart is the only way to grow into the person you aspire to be.

When one is safe within one's core and no longer oscillating from one corner of society to another, the desire to leave behind a unique footprint is manifested in the form of a legacy.

Awareness Is Half the Battle

"Work for a cause, not for applause. Live life to express, not to impress. Don't strive to make your presence noticed, just make your absence felt."

In many respects, this is a revolution. We are all living in an amazing time, almost beyond comprehension. The world is shifting and attitudes are changing, but we must be the catalyst for that change. Self-awareness and knowledge of the current state of the world are the keys to this change. We have come a long way since the era when women couldn't vote and people of certain ethnic backgrounds were considered second-class citizens—but we haven't come far enough.

In today's society, there is still a gender struggle. From media to various professional groups, women are deprived of their rights and treated with inequality. There is an ongoing mental battle that comes from expectations set forth by society, especially amongst those who come from cultures in which women are supposed to be mild and meek.

We feel as though we have to prove our visibility and speak louder for our voices to be heard. We have to demonstrate our talents, to show we are deserving of a life on our own terms. Even those who sacrificed in order to get a good education and forged their own path are challenged to prove their capability and worthiness for leadership positions within companies and organizations.

Many of us believe we could have or be so much more, if only we could make our way through a male-dominated society. But that thought scares us as well. The idea of defying convention can be frightening on multiple levels. This forces some of us to take a back seat and to try to be happy with what we are given.

Not all of us want to be fierce warriors for change; we just want to be on an equal playing field. We'd like to be given the same pay and the same opportunities to lead a life of our own like our male counterparts. Circumstances force us to think small, instead of dreaming big. Sooner or later, culture wins out over individual wants and desires, which causes us to lose bits and pieces of ourselves in the process.

However, around middle age—or sometimes earlier—we begin to question what is "normal" and "expected". We see social injustice for what it truly is, and are able to view the social patterns that define success. We realize these things are structured around systems that make us feel secure. It has nothing to do with fearless perceptions or self-fulfillment, and it is uniquely, or perhaps intrinsically, purpose-driven.

The truth is we all doubt ourselves on a regular basis, and much of that doubt is forced upon us from outside influences. Society shapes our ideas of what is right and wrong, what is acceptable and frowned upon. It governs our lives in many ways, to the point where it hinders our ability to achieve success and happiness. We are all held back by rules that the society and culture have made for us.

The question we ask ourselves at some point in time is: why is the world structured this way? Why is success defined and popularized by a limited definition, and why do we feel the need to adhere to that version of success?

When we ponder these questions, we arrive at a moment of powerful self-discovery and awareness and see that we have allowed it to happen. **We have let culture hinder us, and we have let social trends and media propaganda make us who we are today.**

Isn't it time that we took back control of our lives? Isn't it time to realize we have the power to be anything and anyone we want to be, if only we can grasp the immense strength and courage within us? *No matter which cultural norms exist or what expectations society may have for us, we can lead the lives we are meant to lead!*

Taking Action to Create the Life of Your Dreams

Now that you've gained this knowledge, it's time to put it into action. When the road you are on no longer feels right, even if it has been walked by countless others before you, then you must ask yourself how you are going to forge ahead on your own path. There are those among us who will remain on the sidelines watching life as it dances by and wonder what would have happened if they would have spoken up. They'll think about the lives they could have led, and what they gave up because they weren't willing to claim their true purpose.

Then there are those who will challenge the powerful system and take control of their fates. They will refuse to take the back seat, knowing they are worthy of grabbing the wheel and dictating which road to take. These individuals won't settle for anything less than the best for themselves and for their children. Remember we cannot impose our needs and ambitions on people who may not share them. We must recognize that sources of happiness vary widely between people.

Taking the path of least resistance may be easier. It is less difficult and less stressful to simply go with the flow and never question ourselves. But isn't personal fulfillment and achievement *your* definition of success? Isn't it worth the struggle to leave a legacy of compassion and hope?

Let me leave you with a story that will convey one of the most significant messages of the book. A little girl was watching her mother prepare a fish for dinner. Her mother cut the head and tail off the fish and then placed it into a baking pan. The little girl asked her mother why she cut the head and tail off the fish. Her mother thought for a while and then said, "I've always done it that way—that's how babicka (Czech for grandma) did it."

Not satisfied with the answer, the little girl went to visit her grandma to find out why she cut the head and tail off the fish before baking it. Grandma thought for a while and replied, "I don't know. My mother always did it that way."

So the little girl and the grandma went to visit great-grandma to ask if she knew the answer. Great-grandma thought for a while and said, "Because my baking pan was too small to fit in the whole fish." (Ack M Hamanova)

The little girl did not stop questioning and searched for a reason for conformity. It is up to us to reclaim our inner potential, fearless creativity, and mindfulness. I want to leave you with one final sentiment as we embrace ideas and turn them into action: the road to success is dotted with tempting parking places and unexpected traffic jams. YOU deserve to have an abundant, meaningful, fulfilled, and successful life.

The nine confrontations must be encountered in order to arrive at your unique parking spot of self-awareness and create the map of your value-based culture. You must believe in the power of the universe wanting to deliver your determination, your faith in exercising compassion, and your inner pursuit to question and conquer doubts.

"Our lives have a clear navigation system;
sift the white noise from intuition."

Knowing oneself is paramount in succeeding with one's vision;
So confront yourself head-on and love yourself
for who you truly are.

Design your unique value-based culture map,
so you are confident and worthy to impact the
challenges of work, family, and purpose without regret.

Remember...
"Traditions or norms lose value and purpose, if they
disturb peace in our lives."

Because...
"The role of cultures is to enrich our wisdom, progress,
and ideals in life."

Bibliography

Chapter One.

Well Being Global Success Report, World Economic Forum, 2012,http://www3.weforum.org/docs/WEF_HE_GAC_Wellbeing GlobalSuccess_Report_2012.pdf

Dr. Jeremy Dean, "Conformity: Ten Timeliner Influencers," *PsyBlog, February 16, 2010,* http://www.spring.org.uk/2010/02/conformity-ten-timeless-influencers.php

"Scientists Identify link between size of brain region and conformity," WelcomeTrust, February 21, 2012, http://www.wellcome.ac.uk/News/Media-office/Press-releases/2012/WTVM054438.htm

Chapter Two.

Margarita Tartakovsky, M.S., "5 Ways to Get to Know Yourself Better," *PsychCentral,* reviewed on August 6, 2012, http://psychcentral.com/blog/archives/2012/08/06/5-ways-to-get-to-know-yourself-better/

Sara Canady, "The High Price of Self Awarenessm", *Psychology Today*, October 2, 2013,
http://www.psychologytoday.com/blog/you-according-them/201310/the-high-price-self-awareness

Cordelia Fine, "The Vain Brain," *The Guardian Online*, January 26, 2006,http://www.theguardian.com/theguardian/2006/jan/26/features11.g22

Bradbury, Ray. 1953. *Fahrenheit 451*. New York: Ballantine Books.

Chapter Three.
Nicholas Epley and David Dunning, "Feeling Holier Than Thou: Are Self-Serving Assessments Produced by Errors in Self- or Social Prediction," *Journal of Personality and Social Psychology* 79 (2000): 6, doi: 10.1037//0022-3514.79.6.861

Wendy Wang, Kim Parker, and Paul Taylor, "Breadwinner Moms," *Pew Social Trends*, May 29, 2013,
http://www.pewsocialtrends.org/2013/05/29/breadwinner-moms/.

William F. Fore. 1990. *Mythmakers: Gospel, Culture and the Media*. New York: Friendship Press.

Mark Royal, "Rising Work-Life Balance Concerns Tied to Employee Turnover across the Globe," *Hay Group*, April 16, 2013, http://www.haygroup.com/ww/press/details.aspx?id=36865.

Ray B. Williams, "Wired for Success: How to Fulfill Your Potential," *Psychology Today*, August 18, 2012, http://www.psychologytoday.com/blog/wired-success/201208/im-successful-because-im-beautiful-how-we-discriminate.

John R. Graham, Campbell R. Harvey, and Manju Puri, "A Corporate Beauty Contest," *AFA 2011 Denver Meetings*, Last revised April 9, 2014.

"Arican Village Story" was adapted from story by Dr. Edward Prather - *Emerging Ethnic Engineers Program, University of Cincinnati*

Chapter Four.

Vishen Lakhiani, "Proof of the Vision Board," *Finerminds*, June 15, 2010, http://www.finerminds.com/manifesting/vision-board-john-assaraf/.

A Cimpian, Y Mu, and LC Erickson, "Who is Good at This Game?" *Psychol Sci.* 2012 May 1;23(5):533-41. doi: 10.1177/0956797611429803. Epub 2012 Apr 11.

"Women CEO's of the Fortune 1000," *Catalyst,* June 10, 2014, http://www.catalyst.org/knowledge/women-ceos-fortune-1000

"Redefining Having it All," *Citigroup, Inc,* October 3, 2012, http://www.citigroup.com/citi/news/2012/121003b.htm

Chapter Five.

Alinga Tugend, "Tiptoeing Out of One's Comfort Zone," *The New York Times*, Feburary 11, 2011, http://www.nytimes.com/2011/02/12/your-money/12shortcuts.html?pagewanted=all&_r=0.

Bardwick, Judith M. 1991. *Danger in the Comfort Zone: From Boardroom to Mailroom.* American Management Association.

Yerkes, Robert M. *The dancing mouse.* New York: The Macmillan Company.

Scott Eidelman, Jennifer Pattershall, and Christian S. Crandall, "Longer is Better," *Journal of Experimental Pyschology* 46 (2010): 9, DOI: 10.1016/j.jesp.2010.07.008.

Ran Zilca, "Comfort Kills," *Psychology Today*, January 27, 2011, http://www.psychologytoday.com/blog/confessions-techie/201101/comfort-kills.

Christopher Bergland, "Stepping Outside Your Comfort Zone Keeps Your Sharp," *Psychology Today*, October 22, 2013, http://www.psychologytoday.com/blog/the-athletes-way/201310/stepping-outside-your-comfort-zone-keeps-you-sharp.

Chapter Six.

Jennifer Kromber, PsyD, "4 Difficulties of Being a Perfectionist," *Psychology Today*, November 7, 2013, http://www.psychologytoday.com/blog/inside-out/201311/4-difficulties-being-perfectionist.

Nicholas Epley and David Dunning, "Feeling Holier Than Thou: Are Self-Serving Assessments Produced by Errors in Self- or Social Prediction," *Journal of Personality and Social Psychology* 79 (2000): 6, doi: 10.1037//0022-3514.79.6.861.

Emma Seppala, "Self Compassion: How to Value Yourself,"
Spiritualy ▯ ▯ealth, http://spiritualityhealth.com/articles/self-compassion-how-value-yourself/page/0/2#sthash.kAyZjPQS.dpuf

Chapter Seven.

Kenton Williams, "The Power of Self Reflection," ▯ *ords of* ▯ *ill*,
July 28, 2012, http://www.wordsofwill.com/the-power-of-self-reflection/.

William F. Fore. 1990. *Mythmakers: ▯ospel, Culture and the Media*.
New York: Friendship Press.

"Religion Linked to Happy Life", *BBC News ▯nline*, March 18,
2008, http://news.bbc.co.uk/2/hi/7302609.stm.

Gretchen Reynolds, "How Exercise Can Strengthen the Brain,"
New York Times, September 28, 2011,
http://well.blogs.nytimes.com/2011/09/28/how-exercise-can-strengthen-the-brain/.

Chapter Eight.

Angie LeVan, "Seeing is Believing: The Power of Visualization,"
Psychology Today, December 3, 2009,

http://www.psychologytoday.com/blog/flourish/200912/seeing-is-believing-the-power-visualization.

Barbara Bradley Hagerty, "Prayer May Reshape Your Brain...And Your Reality," *NP⊡ online*, May 20, 2009, http://www.npr.org/templates/story/story.php?storyId=104310 443.

Chapter Nine.

"Why It Matters," *Seeds of Compassion*,
    http://www.seedsofcompassion.org/why/

Emiliana R. Simon-Thomas, "Three Insights From the Cutting Edge of Compassion Research," *⊡reater ⊡ood*, September 7, 2012,http://greatergood.berkeley.edu/article/item/three_insights_from_the_cutting_edge_of_compassion_research

"Compassion, Culture, and Belief," *⊡nfettered Mind*, 2013, http://www.unfetteredmind.org/compassion-culture-and-belief

"A Compassionate Teacher and the Disciple Who Was a Thief," *⊡umamen*, http://aumamen.com/story/a-compassionate-teacher-and-the-disciple-who-was-a-thief

Clifton B. Parker, "Stanford Research: Compassion Aids Well-
Being," *Stanford News*, February 25, 2014,
http://news.stanford.edu/news/2014/february/dalai-lama-
ccare-022514.html

Taylor, Madisyn. "Little Gurus: Learning to Follow", *Daily ⬚M*,
May 30, 2014,
http://www.dailyom.com/articles/2014/43399.html.

About the Author

Dilshad Dayani is the founding president and CEO of the"World Women Global Council," a global platform to empower women by engaging men, who facilitate the power of change. This unique model of advocacy to action-allowing women to be mentors, leaders, and builders of viable support system powers initiatives focused on education and economic sustainability. Her passion for leadership and commitment to the professional development of others make her a "Woman of Action."

Dilshad also serves as the founding Vice-President of advocacy for United States National Commission-UN WOMEN Dallas Chapter. She has also served as a UN correspondent. Her mission and passion to impact disadvantaged communities started at the age of 13, when she tutored victims of child abuse in Pakistan.

From a diversity advocate to a broadcast journalist, she produced research-based, award-winning bilingual radio/ TV talk shows running in its ninth year using media as a tool of mass education. Dr. Dilshad has used traditional technologies to help empower immigrant families address cultural challenges with resource mobilization and communication tools.

She is also the founding president of the **Lead 2 Empower** institute: an impact driven content management body to support sustainable leadership, gender equality, and global diversity content management body.

As an executive coach, she has helped corporations and civil societies align multicultural work force for productivity, diversity trainings, and family balance. An international speaker and activist with 20 years of core work in social responsibility; she has delivered global outreach projects to empower women and resource mobilization.

Dilshad Dayani also serves on local and national advisory boards, including NPR and KERA. She is the president of the National Diversity Council for women, global thought leader for Kappa Delta Pi, and has been a consultant for the UN on several projects. Her accolades range from media and academia to civil societies locally and nationally.

She was honored the distinguished award for "Outstanding Mentor" by Women's International Network, for her untiring efforts as an advocate, diversity coach, community leader, and broadcast journalist for minorities. Crowned "Mrs. Dallas" by United America pageants 2011-2012, she has won the outstanding community service and photogenic awards.

She lives in Dallas, TX with her husband and two adorable sons.

www.thewwgc.org
www.dilshad.info